ACKNOWLEDGEMENTS

I wish to thank Margaret R. Miles for reading the manuscript of this book and writing its preface on May 9th, 2012.

I wish to thank various British photographers both independent of and connected to the English Heritage Trust (which takes care of Rievaulx Abbey and its grounds) who have given me permission to use their recent photographs of Rievaulx Abbey in this book.

I wish to thank Pamela McCallum, my publisher, for her optimism and helpfulness in getting this book published.

I wish to thank Meaghan Thompson and Craig Smith for their excellent technical assistance. I wish to thank Craig Smith for his editorial expertise.

I wish to thank Margaret Studier, Managing Editor of Harvard Theological Review for her gracious friendship over many years and her tireless moral support.

I wish to thank Purna Rodman Conare for his intellectual understanding of Aelred and his times.

I wish to thank Kathleen R. Hollum for her understanding friendship and wise counsel over many years.

I wish to thank Mona Berman for her friendship over many years.

I am grateful to Professor Elie Wiesel for his generous appreciation of my life and work ever since I became one of his students in 1978. I think Aelred would be considered a" righteous Gentile" by Jewish mystics.

I was very fortunate to have known and been loved by the late Mother Teresa (b. 1910 - d.1997). I know that she would have appreciated Aelred of Rievaulx's complete devotion to God and his tireless attempts to help humanity, particularly the suffering poor.

Finally, my grateful thanks to Aelred of Rievaulx whose living words bring daily inspiration to my life and work.

Shuma Chakravarty
Cohasset, MA
August, 2012.

AUTHOR'S NOTE

Shuma Chakravarty is a scholar and writer whose poetry and prose have been published in several anthologies. She has graduate degrees in English Literature (from Simmons College) and theology from Boston University and Harvard University.

Dedication

This book is dedicated to my saintly mother, Uma Devi Chakravarty and to Professor Margaret R. Miles, teacher, scholar, author and mentor to many and to me. Aelred would have cherished them as his spiritual friends.

The Remarkable Humanism of Aelred of Rievaulx (b.1110 — d.1167).

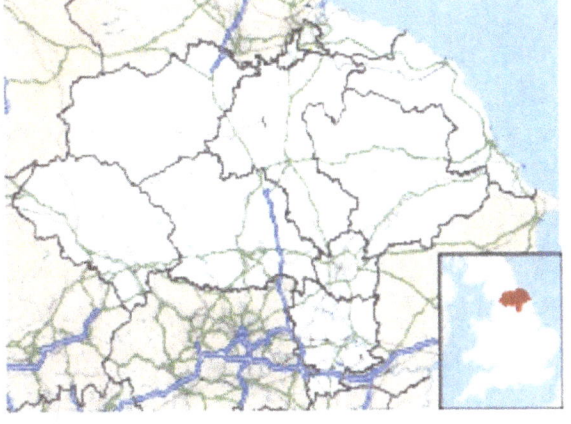

A Celebration of Aelred's Life, Work and Legacy
by
Shuma Chakravarty

ISBN: 978-0-9858282-0-2

Copyright ©2012 Shuma Chakravarty

Published by:
CONVERPAGE
23 Acorn Street
Scituate, MA 02066
www.converpage.com
781-378-1996

Preface

Aelred of Rievaulx, a twelfth-century courtier who became a Cistercian monk, was one of the most generous thinkers of the history of Christianity. In an age when theologians fought fiercely over the correct interpretation of dogma, and warfare between kinsmen and nations ransacked the British Isles, Aelred espoused and practiced humanistic values. In this gem of a book, Shuma Chakravarty places Aelred in his institutional, intellectual, and cultural setting, the better to reveal the uniqueness of his thought among his contemporaries. Aelred was esteemed by his fellow monks who elected him abbot of the large monastery at Rievaulx as well as by later scholars, theologians, and medievalists. Chakravarty's well-researched exploration of Aelred's life and thought reveals the extent of his influence to our own time. For readers familiar with the religious and secular intolerance of Aelred's time, his gentle appreciation of friendship will come as a happy surprise. Although he may have been the most atypical man of his time, Aelred's authorship and example demonstrate the generosity of his spirit in the midst of harsh conflict.

Margaret R. Miles, Emerita Professor of Historical Theology, The Graduate Theological Union, Berkeley, CA. She was the Dean and Vice President of Academic Affairs at The Graduate Theological Union from 1996 until 2001. She was a member of the Harvard Divinity School faculty from 1978 until 1996. In 1985, she became the first woman to receive tenure at Harvard Divinity School. During her years at Harvard Divinity School she held many important positions and was the Bussey Professor of Historical Theology. Since 2000 she has been a member of the Visiting Committee, Harvard University Divinity School and chair of this committee since 2004.
She has received many academic honors and distinctions and is the author of many books and articles.

Author's Notes.

In Memoriam: Mother Teresa (b. 1910 -- d. 1997)

I knew Mother Teresa for many years and I was very fortunate to have been loved by her. She often said: "Do something beautiful for God" and "Do small things with great love." I hope this book on St. Aelred of Rievaulx fulfills those loving injunctions of Mother Teresa. In 1996, I was with Mother Teresa in her headquarters, (known as the Mother House), in Kolkata, India, when these photographs were taken by visitors on several occasions. The various autographed cards were given to me by Mother Teresa. She would have appreciated and understood St. Aelred's complete devotion to God and his tireless efforts to help humanity, especially the suffering poor.

The fruit of SILENCE is Prayer
The fruit of PRAYER is Faith
The fruit of FAITH is Love
The fruit of LOVE is Service
The Fruit of SERVICE is Peace

Mother Teresa

God bless you
Me Teresa mc

LOVE TO PRAY — feel often during the day the need for prayer and take trouble to pray. Prayer enlarges the heart until it is capable of containing God's gift of Himself. Ask and seek, and your heart will grow big enough to receive Him and keep Him as your own.

Dear Shuma

See! I will not forget you . . . I have carved you on the palm of My Hand . . . I have called you by your name . . . You are mine . . . You are precious to Me . . . I love you.

Isaiah

God bless you
M Teresa mc

AUTHOR'S PREFACE

The first version of this book on Aelred of Rievaulx was my dissertation in 1987 which was very well-received by the Harvard Divinity School professors who read it and examined me on this topic. They had encouraged me to publish my thesis at that time. I did not find a suitable publisher then.

Margaret R. Miles needs no introduction. However, I wish to express my profound gratitude to her for the excellent academic guidance that I received from her when I was one of her many students at Harvard Divinity School.

Recently I decided to update my work on Aelred of Rievaulx and I am fortunate to have found a publisher.

In 2010, the 900th birthday of Aelred of Rievaulx was celebrated in Rievaulx Abbey in Yorkshire, England.
This book is a continuation of the celebration of Aelred's life, work and legacy. I agree with John Sentamu, the Archbishop of York whose moving tribute to Aelred is included in this book. He mentions that Aelred's message of loving God and humanity is still of vital importance in the twenty first century.

Instead of including comments on my work by various scholars on the back page, I decided to have the reader see at a glance the tributes to Aelred from church leaders in the U.K., dating from 1167 to 2010.

The physical destruction of Rievaulx Abbey in 1538 by the Duke of Rutland, the consequent dispersion of the monks, the seizing of the assets of Rievaulx by Rutland (which had hitherto been used to help the local population of neighboring villages, specially the disabled and destitute), did not destroy Rievaulx Abbey as a sacred space nor did it erase from the public's mind the memory of Rievaulx Abbey's greatest abbot, Aelred.

Today the ruins of Rievaulx Abbey and the grounds are carefully tended by members of the English Heritage Trust and many people come from near and far to Rievaulx, even now, for pilgrimage and prayer. Local villagers continue the medieval practice of having arts and crafts fairs on the grounds of Rievaulx Abbey. They wear medieval clothes, serve medieval food, demonstrate medieval skills of falconry, pottery, book binding, music and cooking etc. thus maintaining Rievaulx Abbey's tradition of hospitality that dates from Aelred's time as abbot in the twelfth century.

It is my sincere hope that the spiritual radiance, intellectual greatness and emotional generosity of Aelred of Rievaulx will shine through this book and that his message will bring renewed inspiration and hope to us all.

Cum caritas,

Shuma Chakravarty
August, 2012.

900th birthday celebration of Aelred at Rievaulx on April 24th, 2010.

The Archbishop of York, John Sentamu, followed in the footsteps of St. Aelred of Rievaulx, walking from Helmsley Castle to Rievaulx Abbey as part of the site's 900th anniversary celebrations of the birth of the saint.

The Archbishop of York took this two hour walk in the company of many people, retracing the route taken by Aelred when he first visited Rievaulx during a trip to Helmsley Castle.

The trip was followed by a private ceremony at Rievaulx Abbey hosted by the Rev.Christopher Ellis, the event's organizer and founder of the Ecumenical Fellowship of Aelred, in which the ruins of the Abbey echoed with the sound of hymns sung by the assembled congregation and plainsong. Abbot Joseph Delargy addressed the group on "Aelred: Theologian and Spiritual Guide." The Archbishop of York reflected on how Aelred's teachings are still relevant in the 21st century.

The Archbishop of York was joined in the ceremony by members of the clergy, including Abbot Joseph Delargy and monks from the Cistercian, Mount St. Bernard's Abbey in Leicestershire. Sister Dorothy Stella and sisters from St. Hilda's Priory in Whitby, Abbess Andrea Savage and sisters from Stanbrook Abbey in Wass, North Yorkshire and Canon Graham Usher, Rector of Hexham Abbey.

" The Ecumenical Fellowship of Aelred have been hosting small ceremonies at Rievaulx Abbey for several years, but with this key anniversary, we were delighted to help them make it such a memorable occasion," says head of visitor operations for English Heritage, Clea Warner. " When you hear plainsong reverberating around the Rievaulx valley, it really gives you a wonderful impression of how the site would have been during Aelred's tenure -- and it is little wonder that so many people came to Rievaulx Abbey on pilgrimages."

The Ecumenical Fellowship of Aelred was founded in 1993 by the Rev.Christopher Ellis as the then Ecumencial Advisor to the Archbishop of York. The Fellowship is a group of over one hundred people drawn from all Christian denominations through out North Yorkshire. Rev.Ellis comments :" Our focus is to study Christian faith and life together in an atmosphere of mutual respect and enrichment, love and spiritual friendship -- qualities which were at the heart of Aelred's spirituality and his understanding that unity in love between people is the basis for true community. Surely, a lesson for 21st century Britain."

The 900th birthday celebration of Aelred at Rievaulx on April 24th 2010.

The Archbishop of York accompanied by more than a hundred people walked between Helmsley Castle and Rievaulx Abbey in Yorkshire, U.K. on April 24th 2010 to celebrate the 900th birthday of St. Aelred of Rievaulx.

At the end of his walk, the Archbishop of York, John Sentamu, spoke about the atmosphere of Reivaulx Abbey : "You almost feel as if the monks never left here. It's an amazing place !"

"Aelred believed that the love of God is with us all the time and that is the kind of message we desperately need to hear today because if you come from a community where love is being practiced and experienced then there is a chance you can build a much bigger community."

Later in his address, the Archbishop reflected on the relevance of St. Aelred's teaching in the 21st century :

" St. Aelred's teaching of how we should love one another has much to speak to our fractured world today. For we live in a society in which communities have become much weaker. In many cases, people either do not know or trust their neighbors. We have become fearful of the safety of our children. Many older people live alone or in residential homes with little stimulation of friendship.

St. Aelred's faith, so deeply rooted in St. John's teaching, reminds us that we are given the grace and ability to love one another because God first loved us. He also passionately believed the corollary of this which is " If anyone says 'I love God' yet hates their brother or sister, they are liars. For anyone who does not love their brother or sister whom they have seen, cannot love God whom they have not seen."

There is a desperate need in our world today to create this sense that we belong to one another, that we are responsible for each other, and that we should care for one another.

St. Aelred shows us just how we can do this. Our heart, he said, is like a spiritual Noah's Ark made of imperishable wood of virtues and good deeds. In the Noah's Ark of our heart, we should gather and care for all those who are in any kind of need, particularly those who are likely to drown in the chaos of their lives.

Now, it would be wonderful if each of us could take that image away and make it a reality in our lives. Imagine if our hearts could be a spiritual Noah's Ark for all those who are unloved, frightened, lost and in need in our world today. We should include our enemies in our Ark. It may change their hearts, as indeed it will change ours.

My challenge to us all today is to do just that. In our prayers which follow, ask God to help you to identify those He is calling you to put in your Noah's Ark at this time."

The tradition of pilgrimage, prayer and hospitality continues at Rievaulx Abbey.

Rievaulx Abbey continues its tradition of pilgrimage and prayer.

Fr. Mark, MSB "St Aelred Workshop" trip at Rievaulx

Ethiopian monks visited Rievaulx Abbey in 2008.

Pictures of Rievaulx Abbey today

Pictures of Rievaulx Abbey today.

Pictures of Rievaulx Abbey, the village of Rievaulx and the nearby Yorkshire moors.

Current medieval arts and crafts fair on the grounds of Rievaulx Abbey

Current medieval arts and crafts fair on the grounds of Rievaulx Abbey.

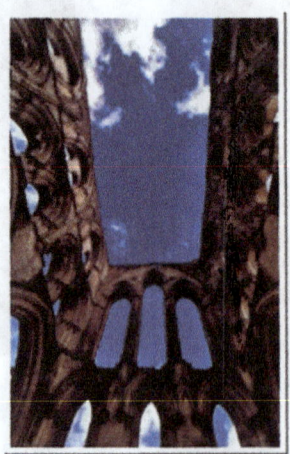

Aelred's emphasis on hospitality continues at Rievaulx Abbey

Aug. 2011

Aug. 2012

Butter making, May 2012

NOTES ON THE PHOTOGRAPHS OF RIEVAULX ABBEY IN THIS BOOK.

The cover page was designed by the author.

The cover page shows what is probably the only surviving medieval representation of Aelred. This picture is from the manuscript of Aelred's *Mirror of Charity*.

Other pictures --The grounds of Rievaulx Abbey had 900 candles on May 19, 2010 to celebrate Aelred's birthday.

The map shows the location of Rievaulx Abbey in Yorkshire, England. A photograph of one of the soaring arches of Rievaulx Abbey which has the effect of a skylight.

The dedication page.

Some of the surviving twelfth century floor tiles from Rievaulx Abbey are now surrounded by grass on the grounds of Rievaulx Abbey. In addition to the medieval sketch of Aelred, there are three recent photographs of Rievaulx Abbey.

The 900th anniversary pictures to celebrate Aelred's birth in 1110, were taken in Rievaulx Abbey on April 24th and May 19th, 2010. The speaker in the photograph is John Sentamu, the Archbishop of York.

This is another picture of the Archbishop of York as he walked, with many others, as a pilgrim from Helmsley Castle to Rievaulx Abbey on April 24th, 2010.

Rievaulx Abbey continues to be a sacred site where people, from near and far, go on pilgrimage. Brother Anthony (Tony Powell of the English Heritage Trust) is offering apples and refreshments to visitors on the grounds of Rievaulx Abbey in 2011.

These are recent photographs of present day pilgrims who visit Rievaulx Abbey.

There is a picture from a prayer book used in Rievaulx Abbey in the 12th century which is now in the British Library in London, U.K.

The river Rye still flows beside Rievaulx Abbey.

The first picture on the medieval fairs page is of a twelfth century tile from Rievaulx Abbey. The other recent pictures show villagers who live near Rievaulx Abbey (in medieval garb) as they demonstrate medieval falconry, pottery, book binding. bagpiping, cooking etc The cottage is in a village near Rievaulx Abbey and is typical of the homes of today's artisans who organize and participate in the current medieval arts and crafts fairs on the grounds of Rievaulx Abbey.

It is interesting to note that even after nine centuries since Aelred's abbacy, the countryside surrounding Rievaulx Abbey is still full of natural beauty and rural charm.

Pictures of Rievaulx Abbey, the village of Rievaulx and the nearby Yorkshire moors.

CONTENTS

Chapter		Page
I.	THE HISTORICAL BACKGROUND.............	1
II.	THE CISTERCIANS IN BRITAIN............	15
III.	SOME NOTIONS AND DEFINITIONS OF THE HUMANISM OF THE TWELFTH CENTURY.......	18
IV.	A BIOGRAPHICAL SKETCH OF AELRED OF RIEVAULX (c. 1110-1167)...............	26
V.	SOME REFLECTIONS ON WALTER DANIEL'S VITA AELREDI...........................	39
VI.	MIRROR OF CHARITY (SPECULUM CARITATIS).............................	52
VII.	"JESUS AT THE AGE OF TWELVE" ("DE JESU PUERO DUODENNI").................	76
VIII.	SPIRITUAL FRIENDSHIP (DE SPIRITUALI AMICITIA).............................	92
IX.	"RULE OF LIFE FOR A RECLUSE" ("DE INSTITUTIONE INCLUSARUM").............	151
X.	SOME RECENT RESPONSES TO THE CONTRIBUTION OF AELRED OF RIEVAULX....	163
APPENDIX	THREE MEDIEVAL LAMENTS................	168
BIBLIOGRAPHY	....	173

CHAPTER I

THE HISTORICAL BACKGROUND

During his lifetime of fifty-seven years, Aelred of Rievaulx (c. 1110-1167) witnessed the reign of three kings in England[1] and four in Scotland.[2]

Aelred was born in c. 1110 when Henry I, a son of William the Conqueror, had already ruled England for a decade. Henry's prudent, though unendearing reign,[3] gave England a period of peace and political stability. Henry I's death in December, 1135 opened the floodgates of anarchy in England. Powerful magnates and barons who had sworn to recognize Henry I's only surviving, legitimate offspring - the Empress Matilda, openly revoked their promise after his demise. Henry I's nephew, Stephen of Blois, hastily arrived in England as soon as he heard of his uncle's death. Contrary to his oath to Henry I (to honor Matilda's claim to the English throne), Stephen was crowned in London, during December, 1135.

Squire informs us that Stephen's

> election by such impressive popular support was confirmed by Pope Innocent II in the spring of the following year, a fact which Stephen is careful to mention, as giving the highest ecclesiastical sanction to his claim, in his charter of liberties of the same spring, 1136.[4]

Although Stephen[5] was described as a likeable and chivalrous man even by those who were his political opponents, he had neither the statesmanship nor the military acumen necessary to win the civil war - a war which rent England from December, 1135 until 1153 when the Treaty of Westminster was signed. By the terms of this treaty between King Stephen and Henry, Duke of Normandy and Anjou, it was agreed that Stephen would continue to reign in England during his lifetime and would be succeeded by Henry whom he adopted as his son and heir. Stephen's eldest son, Eustace, had died in August, 1153, before this treaty was signed. It was also decided and ratified in this treaty that Stephen's younger son, William would inherit all of Stephen's baronial property. The following year, 1154, Stephen died and was succeeded by his appointed heir who ascended the English throne as Henry II, the first of the Plantagenet kings.

Stephen's troubled reign (c. 1135 -54) coincided with a large portion of Aelred's monastic life.[6] Aelred was the anguished witness of the intestine war between kinsmen. To compound his anguish, Aelred's former patron, King David of Scotland, played an important rôle in the disputes during King Stephen's reign.

Soon after Stephen's coronation, King David invaded Northumberland, ostensibly to champion the cause of his niece, Empress Matilda. King David captured all the border castles with the exception of the fortress of Bamborough. David was checked when Stephen advanced to Durham. A treaty of peace was signed at York. David was allowed to keep Carlisle but returned the other castles he had captured. Prince Henry of Scotland (Aelred's childhood friend and the companion of his early youth) was allowed by the terms of the Treaty of York to keep Huntingdon, Carlisle and Doncaster, in exchange for his recognition of Stephen's overlordship in Northumbria. As a reciprocal gesture of amity, Prince Henry of Scotland was given the place of honor at Stephen's Easter court in London in 1136. However, the unfriendly behavior of the Archbishop of Canterbury and some of Stephen's courtiers towards Prince Henry of Scotland, angered King David. He withdrew his son from King Stephen's court and threatened to renew his forays into Northumbria. Furthermore, King David demanded, on Prince Henry's behalf, the earldom of Northumbria (which he alleged had been promised to his son during the peace treaty at York). Stephen refused to accede to this request and David and Henry attacked northern England in 1138. Several contemporary chronicles of this Battle of the Standard exist, the most famous being the accounts of Richard of Hexham, Henry of Huntingdon and Aelred of Rievaulx.

Internal strife[7] in Britain placed Aelred in a situation that must have caused him considerable anguish. Ties of loyalty, affection, and gratitude linked Aelred to the leaders of both sides of the contending armies of the Battle of the Standard which was fought at Northallerton, not far from Rievaulx. Walter Espec was the secular founder of Rievaulx, King David was the patron and mentor of Aelred's pre-monastic life and Prince Henry had been (and still was) one of his closest friends. Moreover, the English and Scottish royal houses were closely knit by the bonds of blood. Professor Powicke observed:

> Ailred, indeed, could not regard the war as an uncompromising conflict between England and Scotland, and still less between Englishmen and Scots. It was a war between kinsmen. David's mother, St. Margaret, was the granddaughter of Edmund Ironside,...but for the verdict of God at Hastings, David would have been the claimant of the legitimist party to the English throne. His sister had been the queen of Henry I, his niece was wife of Stephen, his wife was the daughter of Waltheof, the great earl of Northumberland. If he (David) thought it wise to invade England on behalf of his other niece, the ex-empress Matilda, and try to resume Scottish possession of the northern shires, he could hardly be blamed, though it was doubtless the duty of King Stephen's vassals to resist him. In Ailred's memory the Battle of the Standard was an unhappy conflict of allegiances - for the Bruces and Balliols and other north-country barons had extensive lands in David's domains - and incidentally a revival of that age-long racial struggle of Celt and Teuton.[8]

A peace treaty between England and Scotland was not signed until April, 1139 (the Battle of the Standard was fought in August, 1138). Squire informs us that when this treaty was signed

> King Stephen's position was by that time serious enough to grant Henry (Prince of Scotland) the earldom of Northumberland, which the king had earlier refused. In England the trouble continued for many years yet, but after this David devoted his chief energies to his work for Scotland...[9]

In his description of the Battle of the Standard and in his lament for the demise of King David, Aelred tried to show the merits of Walter Espec and his opponents - King David and Prince Henry of Scotland. One senses the relief with which Aelred welcomed Henry, the great-nephew of King David, to the throne of England in Genealogy of the Kings of England,[10] which he dedicated to the Duke of Normandy in 1153 - a few months before he became Henry II of England.

A medieval source, the Chronicon Petriburgense[11] attributes Henry II's decision to support Cardinal Roland (who became Pope Alexander III in 1159), and not his rival Cardinal Octavian, for the papacy, to the persuasions of Arnulf of Lisieux and Aelred of Rievaulx.

It is interesting to note that the reign of the only English pope in history, Adrian IV[12] (c. 1154-1159), occurred during the abbacy of Aelred of Rievaulx. Aelred had met one of Pope Adrian's predecessors, Pope Innocent II in 1142 when he had visited Rome as a representative of Abbot William of Rievaulx. During this memorable journey Aelred had also met the famous Bernard of Clairvaux who had subsequently ordered him to write his first book The Mirror of Charity

(Speculum Caritatis). Aelred must have experienced no small satisfaction in knowing that a gracious compatriot who had a genuine affection for England and her inhabitants, held the highest rank in Christendom.

However, the former Nicholas Breakspeare's reign as Pope Adrian IV spanned only half a decade.[13] After his death, as mentioned earlier, there were two contenders for the papal throne. The Cistercians ignored the suit of Cardinal Octavian who called himself Pope Victor IV and actively supported Cardinal Roland who became Pope Alexander III. As noted above, Aelred is believed by a medieval source[14] to have persuaded Henry II to support Alexander's claim to the papal chair. In 1161, the new pope expressed his gratitude to the English king by canonizing one of his predecessors and ancestors - Edward the Confessor. Aelred of Rievaulx played a leading role in this event.[15] At the insistence of his kinsman, Laurence of Westminster, Aelred wrote a biography of Edward the Confessor and it is believed by a medieval source (Chronicon Petriburgense) that he delivered the sermon during the celebration of Edward's canonization in Westminster Abbey.

Professor Powicke[16] states that Aelred must have been cognizant of the discord between Henry II and Thomas, Archbishop of Canterbury. Powicke suggests that one of Aelred's letters to Thomas has survived - a letter in which Aelred offered pastoral advice and advocated remembrance of his

ecclesiastical duties. Powicke posits the theory that
Aelred's sympathy probably did not lie in the direction of
Thomas but rather with Gilbert Foliot who was an opponent
of the Archbishop of Canterbury, and a friend of the abbot
of Rievaulx. However, Aelred did not live long enough to
witness the death and posthumous popularity of Thomas

> which turned Becket into St. Thomas of Canterbury,
> and gave him a place even above St. Cuthbert and
> St. Edward the Confessor in the hearts of Englishmen.[17]

Circumstances in Scotland (a country which he visited
periodically) also caused Aelred both anguish and anxiety.
He visited his former patron King David of Scotland during
Lent, 1153, shortly before David's demise. Prince Henry
of Scotland, Aelred's "cradle companion" and the close friend
of his early youth had died in 1152, causing his father, his
country and Aelred grave concern about the future of Scotland.
Aelred fervently hoped that Scotland, like England, would not
be subjected to a disputed succession and the perils of civil
war and anarchy. In his lament for King David, Aelred pleaded[18]
with the Scottish nobility to respect the right of David's
eleven year old grandson Malcolm to the throne of Scotland.
Malcolm[19] did, in fact, succeed his grandfather to the Scottish
throne and reigned from the age of eleven until his early
demise at the age of twenty-four. He was succeeded by his
brother whose prowess earned him the title - William the
Lion.[20]

It is interesting to note that during Aelred's lifetime England was, in several ways, a satellite[21] of France.

Though somewhat lengthy, Southern's cogent analysis is worth quoting in this context. Southern states that

> The Continental connection dominated English government throughout the twelfth century. Nearly everything that happened in English government either stemmed from or was influenced by this basic fact. From the point of view of her Norman or Angevin kings England had two main functions: it gave them a royal title which made them the equals of the greatest rulers of Europe, and it provided them with a base from which they could operate on the Continent. They were mesmerized by the prospect of Continental glory. This may seem a strange miscalculation when we consider how much more might have been won in Ireland, Scotland and Wales at a fraction of the cost of maintaining the Continental connection. But these peripheral countries interested the kings of England only intermittently so long as they had a foothold on the Continent. For that matter England itself scarcely interested them. The great governmental development in England during the century (i.e. the twelfth century) was a token, not of their interest, but their lack of interest in England. It is very doubtful whether the kings had any policy at all in England; they had only expedients for furthering a policy elsewhere. To preserve and extend the Norman and Angevin family inheritance; to press on into the south of France, even perhaps into Italy; to support allies in Flanders and the Rhineland; these were the great objects of the English kings. For these objects they were prepared to take every kind of risk. The variations in their personal character made very little difference: a prudent king like Henry I deviated from all the normal rules of his far-sighted government to seize and keep Normandy; a wise king like Henry II quarrelled with all his family to avoid any diminution of his Continental lordship; even John was willing to rouse and ruin himself in pursuing an impossible policy of restoring his position in France; and so it went on almost to the end of the Middle Ages...Academically, as well as in the mores of aristocratic life, England was a colony of the intellectual empire of France, and its colonial status was emphasized by the fact that, while nearly every English scholar of distinction went to France to study, and often did not return, no distinguished French scholar came to England either to study or to teach...

> ...It was another mark of England's colonial status that it produced the raw materials...and the manufacturing power which processed them, was concentrated abroad...Not only in politics, but in aristocratic social life and culture, in its economic system and its ecclesiastical organization, England was joined to the Continent. It was an integral but subordinate part of a western European order.[22]

In spite of the fact that France was culturally and economically superior to England during the twelfth century, Britain did produce some remarkable[23] persons during this century who were not inferior in any way to their distinguished counterparts across the Channel. Aelred of Rievaulx certainly deserves to be regarded as one of England's chief contributions to the luminaries of this remarkable century. Although Southern regards Aelred as a "figure of mainly local interest,"[24] the Abbot of Rievaulx has received a different evaluation from another twentieth century English historian (David Knowles) whose scholarly reputation is at least as "solid" as that of Southern. Professor Knowles' research has indicated the seminal importance of Aelred during the "renaissance of the twelfth century."[25] Knowles also regards Rievaulx (in Yorkshire, England) during Aelred's abbacy, as a centre of great cultural importance during the twelfth century.

> Here indeed, far from the familiar centres of European life, is the quintessence of the humanism of the twelfth century; Ailred, the novice-master and teacher, surrounded by a small group of finely educated young minds absorbed in living debates - Ailred, the friend and guide, learning recollection and true charity from his contact with others - Ailred the abbot, in middle age and in premature old age brought on by long and sharp illness, the centre of an ever shifting gathering of his sons to whom he,

with his old charm intensified by suffering and sanctity, was all things to all, now discussing the nature of the soul in a dialogue left unfinished at his death, now counselling an illiterate lay-brother with equal care, while around him the fixed life of choir and farm-work of changeless routine and sparing diet, went on unchanged...[26]

...His unique position as a writer - wholly unique in England, and without exact parallel abroad - is due in part to the limpid sincerity with which he laid bare, in his wish to help others, the growth and progress of his own mind and heart from the human to the divine, and in part to the candid humanism of his most characteristic pages.[27]

Notes to CHAPTER I

1. Henry I (1100-1135), Stephen (1135-1154), Henry II (1154-1189). Aelred lived until 1167. Consequently, he witnessed only the first thirteen years of Henry II's long reign.

2. Alexander I (1107-1124), David I (1124-53), Malcolm (1153-1165), William (1165-1214). Aelred witnessed only two years of William of Scotland's reign.

3. See John Gillingham's assessment of Henry I in The Lives of the Kings and Queens of England, ed. by Antonia Fraser (New York: Alfred A. Knopf, Inc., 1975), p. 39:

    Although he ruled England for thirty-five years few English kings are as little known as Henry I. Careful, sober, harsh and methodical he chose his servants from men of a similar stamp. When compared with Rufus and Ranulf Flambard, Henry I and Roger of Salisbury are drab and colorless characters. But from 1102 until the end of his reign there was no revolt in England. A king who could keep the peace for over thirty years was a master of the art of government.

3. See R. W. Southern's evaluation of Henry I in chapter xi, *Medieval Humanism and Other Studies* (Oxford: Basil Blackwell, 1970), pp. 206-233.

4. Aelred Squire, *Aelred of Rievaulx - A Study* (Kalamazoo, Michigan: Cistercian Publications, 1981), p. 75.

5. See John Gillingham's essay on Stephen in *The Lives of the Kings and Queens of England*, pp. 39-43.

   See R. W. Southern's comments on Stephen and his troubled reign in *Medieval Humanism and Other Studies*, pp. 149-150.

6. Aelred became a member of Rievaulx in 1134 and remained a Cistercian until his demise in 1167.

7. See Aelred Squire's chapter entitled "Knights and Kings" in *Aelred of Rievaulx - A Study*, pp. 72-97.

   Also see Andrew Lang's *A History of Scotland*, Volume I (New York: Dodd, Mead, and Co., 1901), pp. 102-109.

8. See F. M. Powicke's introduction to Walter Daniel's *Vita Ailredi* (Oxford: Clarendon Press, 1978), pp. xlvi-xlvii.

9. See Aelred Squire, *Aelred of Rievaulx - A Study*, p. 81.

10. *Ibid.*, pp. 87-91.

11. See F. M. Powicke's introduction to the *Vita Ailredi*, p. xlviii.

12. See R. W. Southern's essay on Pope Adrian IV in chapter xii of his *Medieval Humanism and Other Studies*, pp. 234-252.

    Also see C. H. Haskins' *The Renaissance of the Twelfth Century* (Cambridge: Harvard University Press, 1933), pp. 245-246.

13. Pope Adrian IV (1154-1159).

14. *Chronicon Petriburgense*. Also see Aelred's *Spiritual Friendship (De Spirituali Amicitia)*, (Kalamazoo, Michigan: Cistercian Publications, 1977), pp. 79-80.

15. See Aelred Squire, *Aelred of Rievaulx - A Study*, pp. 94-97.

16. See F. M. Powicke's introduction to the Vita Ailredi, pp. xlix-li.

17. Ibid., p. li.

18. "But (says Aelred in his lament) the age of a king is to be measured by the faith of his knights. Pay the sons what you owed the father; let them find you grateful for the benefits you received. Moreover, let the perils of the English teach you to keep faith with kings, to preseve mutual concord among yourselves, lest foreigners devour your land before you, and it be laid waste as in the devastation of war."

    Translated into English (from Aelred's medieval Latin lament for King David I of Scotland) by A. Squire. See Squire's Aelred of Rievaulx - A Study, p. 86.

19. Malcolm of Scotland reigned from 1153 until his early demise in 1165. Endowed with great physical and inner beauty, he was nicknamed, "Malcolm the Maiden." Crowned at the age of eleven, this youthful monarch died when he was twenty-four years old. His brother William succeeded him to the throne.

20. Andrew Lang's A History of Scotland, Volume I, (pp. 108-119) provides a responsible synopsis of the reigns of Malcolm and William - the grandsons of King David I of Scotland.

21. See R. W. Southern's Medieval Humanism and Other Studies, pp. 158-159:

    "Culturally the most obvious thing about England in the twelfth century is its dependence on France. It was a colony of the French intellectual empire, important in its way and quite productive, but still subordinate. Scholars, poets, architects and religious reformers in England did the same things as their contemporaries in France, rather less well, and in a provincial and derivative way. England made no great, distinctive contribution in any of the fields which are the special glory of the twelfth century. Among teachers of the liberal arts there is no name in England to put beside those of William of Conches, Thierry of Chartres, and Petrus Helias; there is no theologian to put beside Abelard, Peter Lombard, Hugh of St. Victor, Peter of Poitiers and Peter the Chanter; no canon lawyer to compare with Gratian, Huguccio, or Bernard of Pavia; no one in the same class as Chrétien of Troyes in vernacular poetry, or Walter of Chatillon, Hugh Primas and the Archpoet in Latin; among monastic legislators only Gilbert of Sempringham has a place - a very modest one - beside the founding fathers of Carthusian, Cistercian, and Augustinian Orders. In architecture there is no great seminal building like the church of St. Denis. The Crusade fell on dull ears in England until the least English of her kings infused some life into a long-delayed project.

Naturally this admission of inferiority will arouse some protests. In the liberal arts it may be said that if England has no William of Conches, at least it has John of Salisbury. But this objection is not as conclusive as it sounds. John wrote in England, but everything that he wrote he had learnt in France. Then again, he was not a teacher of liberal arts in England, but a failed academic driven into administration by lack of scholarly opportunities. His case will deserve some attention later, but it does not modify our first judgement. The same may be said about the line of distinguished theologians - Robert Pullen, Robert of Melun, Stephen Langton - who, if not in the same class as Abelard and Peter Lombard, nevertheless made a considerable contribution to the development of the subject. They were all men who went to France to learn their trade and make their careers as teachers, because they found no sufficient opportunities in England. Similarly, the leading English canon lawyers like Alanus, Gilbertus, Richardus Anglicus and Gerard Pucelle all studied and taught abroad, at Bologne and Paris. The same answer would have to be given to anyone who mentions Stephen Harding among monastic legislators. Certainly the English legislator of Citeaux was among the greatest religious figures of the century - but not in England. He crossed the sea for inspiration and converted no single house or man in England.

It would be foolish to say that nothing of interest was produced in England in these fields of activity. In theology we can point to the works of the group of pupils of St. Anselm, or to the Isagoge in Theologiam of an unknown pupil of Abelard who seems to have written his work after his return to England. In law, there is Vacarius at Oxford, and later there are the decretal collections which seem to have been made in English schools. At this modest level of achievement a quite impressive list of works

of theology and law produced in England in the
twelfth century could be drawn up; but they would
only emphasize the derivative and subordinate
character of the English contribution to these
subjects."

22. Ibid., pp. 138-140. Although Southern concludes his investigation about the somewhat inferior rank of England in the twelfth century with a statement (p. 180) that England was not, after all, "a colony of the French intellectual empire," his previous evidence and arguments about the satellite status of England during this period are more convincing than his denial.

23. Henry Murdac, Waldef, Aelred of Rievaulx, Stephen Harding, Richard of Fountains, John of Salisbury, Robert Pullen, Robert of Melun, Stephen Langton, Alanus, Gilbertus, Richardus Anglicus, Gerard of Pucelle, Lawrence of Westminster, Gilbert of Hoiland and Jocelin of Furness - to mention but a few remarkable Englishmen of the twelfth century.

24. See Southern, Medieval Humanism and Other Studies, pp. 159-160.

25. See C. H. Haskins' The Renaissance of the Twelfth Century.

26. See David Knowles' "The Humanism of the Twelfth Century," in The Historian and Character (Cambridge: The University Press, 1963), p. 26.

27. Please see David Knowles' The Monastic Order in England, (Cambridge: The University Press, 1950), p. 265.

CHAPTER II

THE CISTERCIANS IN BRITAIN

The first half of the twelfth century witnessed the phenomenal growth of the Cistercian order under the magnetic leadership of Bernard of Clairvaux. A group of Englishmen from Yorkshire[1] were close associates of the famous Bernard and it is probable that it was at their vigorous suggestion that Yorkshire was "chosen for the first transmarine foundation of Clairvaux."[2]

Both Henry I[3] of England and his brother-in-law, David of Scotland[4] were very hospitable to religious orders who received both financial help and protection from their royal patrons.

Bernard of Clairvaux tactfully sent a letter to Henry I in 1131 and chose his English secretary William to lead the Cistercians whom he sent to Yorkshire.[5] The Cistercians founded Rievaulx in Yorkshire, in 1132.

Knowles informs us, however, that

> ...The distinction of first introducing the white monks (Cistercians) to England belongs, not to Thurstan and Clairvaux, but to L'Aumone and William Giffard of Winchester. The site chosen was Waverley, near Farnham in Surrey, in what was then a somewhat remote locality away from the main lines of travel. The abbot and community from L'Aumone were presumably foreigners, and settled down unostentatiously to their regular life at the end of 1128. Waverly though it grew steadily and made a number of foundations, attracted no recruits of renown, and Ailred, perhaps with a touch of patriotic bias, could speak of it as hidden away in a corner. The foundation that truly marked the beginning of the invasion was that of Rievaulx, near Helmsley, some thirty miles north of York. The founder was Walter Espec, acting in close concert with Thurstan (Archbishop of York)...[6]

The period from 1132 to 1152 witnessed the rapid growth of Cistercian foundations in England. Knowles observed:

> The year 1147, in which the affiliation of Savigny to Citeaux was effected, witnessed a greater number of Cistercian foundations in England - seven in all - than any year before or after. It was besides the year in which Henry Murdac became archbishop of York, and Ailred abbot of Rievaulx. It marked, indeed, in many ways the apogee of the new order considered as a force working upon the Church and society.
>
> The summer solstice of Cistercian growth was not of long continuance. It came to an abrupt end some six years later, when the prohibition by general chapter of...foundations in the future was followed within a year by the deaths of the Cistercian pope (Eugenius III) and of the abbot of Clairvaux. As regards England the year 1152 marks, for all practical purposes, the end of the era of propagation...Wales, however... received its quota of white monk foundations in the fifty years which followed.[7]

Notes to CHAPTER II

1. See David Knowles' The Monastic Order in England, pp. 228-229:

   From the outset Englishmen had been found among the groups of reformers abroad, and the fame of Stephen Harding must have served as an attraction to his countrymen. We do not know when the first Englishman entered Clairvaux, but William, the future first abbot of Rievaulx, must have been there in very early years, for he was Bernard's amanuensis for the celebrated letter to his nephew, Robert of Chatillon, c. 1116-19. It is possible that he is to be identified with the William, a pupil of Henry Murdac at York, who joined with Ivo, a fellow-pupil and later a fellow-monk at Clairvaux, in saluting their old master, to whom Bernard addressed the eloquent invitation quoted in the preceding chapter. Murdac, as is well known, responded and became one of the most distinguished Cistercians of the age. If the suggested identification be not correct, there were two Englishmen named William at Clairvaux, and the second may also have returned later to his native country. Ivo, for his part, persuaded Bernard to write to another friend, Thomas, the young provost of Beverley, inviting him to leave all and become a monk. Thomas promised, but in spite of a second long and warm letter failed to keep his word. Yet another northerner of distinction to find a home at Clairvaux was Richard, a native of York, who after following Henry Murdac as third abbot of Vauclair, succeeded him again as sixth abbot of Fountains; and mention has already been made of Philip, the prebendary of Lincoln. Circumstances had thus brought it about that among Bernard's most trusted disciples was a small group from York and its neighbourhood...

2. Ibid., p. 229.

3. See R. W. Southern's Medieval Humanism and Other Studies, p. 232.

4. See A. Squire's Aelred of Rievaulx - A Study, p. 85.

5. See David Knowles' The Monastic Order in England, chapter xiii, pp. 227-245.

6. Ibid., p. 230.

7. Ibid., p. 252.

CHAPTER III

SOME NOTIONS AND DEFINITIONS OF THE
HUMANISM OF THE TWELFTH CENTURY

The phrase "medieval humanism" may sound like a contradiction in terms to modern, post-Renaissance minds. The medieval notions of man as mortal, subservient to the omnipotent will of God, in obedience to his/her feudal leiges and ecclesiastical superiors and humbly occupying his/her preordained place in the social hierarchy are hardly consonant with our concepts of "humanism." The Renaissance sense of wonder[1] at the magnificence of mortals, awe evoked by our astonishing powers of creativity and capacity for delight in the beauty and pleasures of nature and of this world - this enthusiastic applause seems to merit the name of "humanism."

The terms "Renaissance" and "the fifteenth and sixteenth centuries" were long synonymous. However, recent historians have carefully re-examined the word "Renaissance" and there is no longer an immediate and exclusive equation of that term with the fifteenth and sixteenth centuries in Europe. In 1840, J.-J.-A. Ampère in his <u>Histoire littéraire de la France avant le douzième siecle</u> wrote:

> I maintain that there were three renaissances: the first dates from Charlemagne; the second which falls at the end of the eleventh century, initiates the Middle Ages; the last is the great renaissance of the fifteenth and sixteenth centuries.[2]

Moreover, in the twentieth century, the responsible research of Haskins,[3] Chenu,[4] Bouyer,[5] Knowles[6] and Southern[7] has contributed significantly to a clearer understanding of Anglo-European medieval history.

Haskins' <u>The Renaissance of the Twelfth Century</u> was published in 1927. This pioneering work did much to displace the equation of the Renaissance with the fifteenth and sixteenth centuries popularized by Burckhardt (1860) and Voigt (1859).[8] It may not be an exaggeration to suggest that Haskins prepared the ground for the subsequent contributions to and discussions of the topic of the Renaissance by such scholars as Ferguson, Sanford, Holmes and Chenu.[9]

Haskins' careful scholarship indicated that

> ...modern research shows us the Middle Ages less dark and less static, the Renaissance less bright and less sudden than was once supposed. The Middle Ages exhibit life and color and change, much eager search after knowledge and beauty, much creative accomplishment in art, in literature, in institutions. The Italian Renaissance was preceded by similar, if less wide-reaching movements; indeed it came out of the Middle Ages so gradually that historians are not agreed when it began and some would go so far as to abolish the name,

and perhaps even the fact, of a renaissance in the Quattrocento.

> ...The Renaissance of the Twelfth Century...is often called the Medieval Renaissance. This century...was in many respects an age of fresh and vigorous life. The epoch...of the rise of towns, and of the earliest bureaucratic states of the West, it saw the culmination of Romanesque art and the beginnings of Gothic; the emergence of the vernacular literatures; the revival of the Latin classics and of Latin poetry and Roman law; the recovery of Greek science, with its Arabic additions, and of much of Greek philosophy; and the origin of the first European universities. The twelfth century left its signature on higher education, on the scholastic philosophy, on European systems of law, on architecture and sculpture, on the liturgical drama, on Latin and vernacular poetry.[10]

Professor David Knowles' analysis of the characteristics of the humanism of the twelfth century is also cogent and worth quoting. In *The Historian and Character*, Knowles observed that

> The three notes of the new humanism, which set the great men and women of the eleventh and twelfth centuries apart from those who had gone before and who came after, may be put out as: first, a wide literary culture; next, a great and what in the realm of religious sentiment would be called a personal devotion to certain figures of the ancient world; and, finally, a high value set upon the individual, personal emotions, and upon the sharing of experiences and opinions within a small circle of friends.
>
> ...The men of the early twelfth century, if they are regarded with attention and sympathy, show themselves as possessed of a rare delicacy of perception and warmth of feeling...
>
> The hall-mark of the revival, and the accomplishment that was most widely possessed by all whom it affected, was a capability of self-expression based on a sound training in grammar and a long and often loving study of the foremost Latin writers...And though the luminous and adequate expression of ideas and emotions does not of itself alone constitute a character which we

call humanist - for neither Anselm nor Bernard, past
masters of the craft of letters, are precisely humanists -
yet, the power of self-expression grounded upon, or
at least reinforced by, a wide literary culture is a
condition <u>sine qua non</u> of a humanists's growth.[11]

As suggested earlier, the responsible research of scholars such as Haskins and Knowles paved the way for Southern's excellent exposition of aspects of medieval history in his <u>Medieval Humanism</u>.

Excerpts from <u>Medieval Humanism</u> cannot, of course, do more than give a hint of Southern's detailed and engagingly lucid analysis of the humanism of the Middle Ages. However, it may be pertinent in this context to quote some of Southern's comments on medieval humanism.

> What are the symptoms which will establish the existence
> of a deep-seated humanism in the period we are to study?
> I take them to be these:
>
> In the first place there can be no humanism without
> a strong sense of the dignity of human nature...That man
> is a fallen creature, that he has lost his immediate
> knowledge of God, that his instincts and reason are often
> in conflict, and that he is radically disorganized and
> disoriented - all this is common ground to all Christian
> thinkers. We must not expect a denial of these facts
> in the Middle Ages, or even for that matter in the Ren-
> aissance; but we may expect a humanist to assert not
> only that man is the noblest of God's creatures, but
> also that his nobility continues even in his fallen state,
> that it is capable of development in this world, that the
> instruments exist by which it can be developed, and that
> it should be the chief aim of human endeavour to perfect
> these instruments.
>
> Along with this large view of man's natural dignity there
> must go a recognition of the dignity of nature itself.
> This second feature of humanism is a consequence of the
> first, for if man is by nature noble, the natural order
> itself of which he forms a part, must be noble. The two
> are linked together by indissoluble ties and the power
> to recognize the grandeur and splendour of the universe

is itself one of the greatest expressions of the grandeur and splendour of man. Thus man takes his place in nature; and human society is seen as part of the grand complex of the natural order bound together by laws similar to those which tie all things into one.

Finally, the whole universe appears intelligible and accessible to human reason: nature is seen as an orderly system, and man - in understanding the laws of nature - understands himself as the main part, the key-stone, of nature. Without this understanding it is hard to see how men can experience that confidence in human powers which humanism implies.

When those elements of dignity, order, reason and intelligibility are prominent in human experience, we may reasonably describe as humanistic the outlook which ensues. This humanism will be much nearer to the type I have described as "scientific" than to "literary" humanism, but I believe that this must be our starting point in any study of the central period of the Middle Ages.

The starting point is important because the subject has been confused by the tendency to start with the humanism of the Renaissance. This has given the love of ancient literature and the ability to imitate the style of ancient authors an exaggerated importance in judging medieval humanism...

...To begin with man and nature and to find in them the road to God is very characteristic of the new age (i.e. the late eleventh and twelfth centuries)...This search for man was at first a monastic programme, and it was in the monasteries also that another aspect of human experience began to be appreciated - the experience of friendship. Without the cultivation of friendship there can be no true humanism. If self-knowledge is the first step in the rehabilitation of man, friendship - which is the sharing of this knowledge with someone else - is an important auxiliary...

...Of all the forms of friendship rediscovered in the twelfth century, there was none more eagerly sought than the friendship between God and man...

...By 1160 Aelred of Rievaulx was able to sum up the results of the monastic experience of the past century in the words "Friendship is wisdom," *amicitia nihil aliud est quam sapientia*, or even "God is friendship," *Deus est amicitia*. He was careful to say that these

phrases had to be accepted with some reserve, but they
expressed the close relationship between human friendship and the nature of God. The experience of friendship
lay along the road to God. Nature, said Aelred, makes
man desire friendship, experience fortifies it, reason
regulates it, and the religious life perfects it.
So here again we start with nature and end with God.
The treatise that Aelred wrote on friendship is the
most beautiful example of the casting of an ancient
humanistic theme into a Christian mould, and the sequence
which it elaborates - nature prompting, reason regulating,
experience strengthening, religion perfecting - is the
basis of all religious humanism.[12]

Aelred's medieval humanism differs greatly, of course, from that of the ancient Greeks. Fearful of the jealous wrath of their capricious gods, their terrible exactions for the sin of pride, the earliest "humanists" of the western world - the ancient Greeks - felt a profound sense of disquiet about the human condition. Sophocles wrote: "Call no man happy until he is dead." Heraclitus praised man but was poignantly aware of the brevity of mortals' lives. In a daring epigram he wrote: "What then are gods? Men who are immortal. What then are men? Gods who are mortal."

Medieval writers of the fourteenth century expressed an increasingly pessimistic, even bleak view of the human condition. The humanists of the Renaissance of the fifteenth and sixteenth centuries sought solace by belonging to a small group of "cultured" friends[13] with whom they could nostalgically discuss the vanished glories of the classical world. Medieval humanism reached is apex in the fine flowering of the twelfth century when Aelred and his contemporaries, both in the religious and in the secular world, felt a renewed sense of the wonder and worth of the "infinite variety" of human nature[14] and its environment.

Notes to CHAPTER III

1. "What a piece of work is man! How noble in reason! How infinite in faculty! In form and moving how express and admirable! In action how like an angel! In apprehension how like a god! The beauty of the world! The paragon of animals!..."

   Shakespeare, *Hamlet*, Act II, Sc. ii.

2. Quoted by M.-D. Chenu in *Nature, Man, and Society in the Twelfth Century* (Chicago: The University of Chicago Press, 1968), p. 1.

3. C. H. Haskins, *The Renaissance of the Twelfth Century*, (Cambridge: Harvard University Press, 1933).

4. See n. 2, above.

5. Louis Bouyer, *The Cistercian Heritage* (London: A. R. Mowbray and Co., Ltd., 1958), pp. 125-160. Chapter VI of this book is a cogent essay on Aelred of Rievaulx.

6. See David Knowles' "The Humanism of the Twelfth Century" in *The Historian and Character* (Cambridge: The University Press, 1963), pp. 16-30.

7. R. W. Southern, *Medieval Humanism and Other Studies* (Oxford: Basil Blackwell, 1970).

8. See Chenu's *Nature, Man and Society in the Twelfth Century*, p. 1.

9. *Ibid.*, p. 3, n. 3.

10. Haskins, *The Renaissance of the Twelfth Century*, pp. vii-viii.

11. Knowles, "The Humanism of the Twelfth Century", pp. 19-20.

12. Southern, *Medieval Humanism and Other Studies*, pp. 31-32, pp. 34-35.

13. *Ibid.*, p. 60.

14. Squire, *Aelred of Rievaulx - A Study*, pp. 41-43.

CHAPTER IV

A BIOGRAPHICAL SKETCH OF
AELRED OF RIEVAULX (c. 1110-1167)

Aelred came from an ancient Northumbrian family[1] which, for generations, played an active rôle in the ecclesiastical and educational life of northern England.

Aelred's great-grandfather was Alfred, son of Westou. Alfred was the "keeper" of the tomb of the venerated St. Cuthbert. Alfred's son, Aelred's grandfather, was Eilaf, a *larwa* (teacher) and a married priest. His son, another Eilaf was Aelred's father who continued the family tradition of hereditary priesthood coupled with marriage and family life.

The Norman rulers and the French clergy who controlled England during this period wished to root out married priests of the old (i.e. Anglo-Saxon) order, reinstate a celibate clergy and implement the Gregorian reforms.

At the end of his life, Aelred's father Eilaf accepted the new movement of Norman reform and became a monk during his final illness. This event was witnessed by his three sons, one of whom (Aelred) was already a monk of the Cistercian order.

Aelred was born in c. 1110 at Hexham in northern England and probably received his early education at Durham either from his father or from his uncle, Aldred. Aelred always had a deep affection for this geographic area and its ancient religious tradition. He wrote about the saints of Hexham and a book about St. Cuthbert was dedicated to Aelred by Reginald of Durham.

Although the precise date is not known, during his boyhood, Aelred was sent to a distinghished "finishing school" - the court of King David I of Scotland.

King David I[2] had many close links with the ruling house of England and the nobles of Northumbria. His mother, St. Margaret was a granddaughter of Edmund Ironside, a direct descendant of Alfred the Great of England. David's sister Matilda was the first wife of Henry I of England. One of his nieces was Empress Matilda, Henry I's designated heiress to the English throne. His other niece, another Matilda was the wife of King Stephen of England. Moreover, David's wife was the daughter of Waltheof, the Earl of Northumberland.

Squire informs us that though

> Born a Scot, David had been brought up in England in the household of Henry I and his own sister, Henry's sophisticated, francophile Queen Matilda...To David

the Norman way was the normal way to do things and it was natural that he should see to it that his stepson Waldef spoke French as well as he spoke English.[3]

Aelred considered himself an Englishman[4] in the Normanized, Scottish court of David I. However, he received many social, educational and religious advantages in Scotland which helped to deepen and broaden his perspective. As King David's steward,[5] he was responsible for the smooth "functioning" of the royal meals and banquets. Aelred was a favored courtier of David I and a close friend of both his son Prince Henry[6] (whom Aelred once described as his "cradle companion") and his step-son Waldef,[7] who preceded Aelred into monastic life and who remained his lifelong friend and companion.

Squire has observed that

> ...under the discerning patronage of King David, his (i.e. Aelred's) life expanded in an atmosphere of friendship. The adaptation to Norman ways which had been so long and difficult a process for his father (Eilaf), and so late and so imperfectly accomplished, was made easy for him at the court of this king... This, then, became the normal (i.e. Norman), world for Aelred...the world he could more easily take for granted than the one into which he had been born, since he was absorbing its new values at a time when the mind is most impressionable and in the company of men, the memory of whom always remained...dear...in his life...[8]

> In a time of change, when self-awareness was an asset, Aelred was by family and birth intimately connected with the still vital traditions of the past, while in politics and religion he was identified with all that was new. In his personal development old and new conduct an amicable dialogue.[9]

Walter Daniel, Aelred's first biographer, tells us in his <u>Vita Ailredi</u>[10] that Aelred was held in high esteem in the Scottish court and was on the brink of a very distinguished career when he decided to become a Cistercian novice.

In his Mirror of Charity (Speculum Caritatis) Aelred informs his readers that he was inwardly restless and unhappy although he enjoyed many privileges and advantages in the hospitable milieu of King David's court.

> And those men who were around me, but who were ignorant of the things which went on within me, kept saying, 'How lucky he is, how lucky he is,' But they did not know that there was evil in me where only good should be. Terrible was the distress I felt within myself, tormenting me, corrupting my soul with intolerable stench. And unless you had quickly stretched out your hand, not being able to tolerate myself, I might have taken the most desperate remedy of despair.[11]

In 1134, at the age of twenty-four, Aelred was sent by King David of Scotland to Northumbria. Professor Powicke informs us that

> He (i.e. Aelred) was sent on the king's business to Archbishop Thurston of York. For many years the claim of the archbishop to be the metropolitan of the Scottish bishoprics had met with opposition, especially from John, bishop of Glasgow. In spite of papal injunctions the bishop was still disobedient in 1135-6. It was doubtless on some errand arising out of this dispute that Aelred, about 1134, made the journey from which he did not return. On his way home he entered the abbey of Rievaulx.[12]

One of the foremost Aelredian scholars of the twentieth century, A. Squire,[13] suggests that Aelred's boyhood friend Waldef was probably the first to tell him about the advent of the Cistercians in England. In 1134, Waldef was a prior of the canons of Kirkhan and probably told Aelred that Archbishop Thurston was the most appropriate person to give him a letter of introduction to Walter Espec of Helmsley - a great patron of the Cistercians in Yorkshire.

Walter Daniel informs us that Aelred visited Rievaulx after spending a night in Walter Espec's castle. Walter Daniel has also left us a vivid description[14] of the powerful attraction that Rievaulx immediately exercised on Aelred. However, true to his modest, equable nature, Aelred had extended his gracious deference to a subordinate.[15] Aelred had asked him whether he wished to pay a second visit to Rievaulx. When the man agreed to do so, Aelred returned to Rievaulx and decided to join the Cistercian community. With the exception of one person (other than Aelred), in the group of men who had come with him from Scotland on their "king's business", all the others returned north to the Scottish court.

The next eight years (1134-1142) were crucially important[16] in Aelred's life. It was during this formative period that Aelred transformed himself from a courtier into a contemplative, from a royal steward into a manual laborer. Walter Daniel has left us a vivid vignette of Aelred's cheerful willingness to adapt himself to the rigor and vicissitudes of the Cistercian way of life.

> He (Aelred) approached every action without delay, pride or reluctance; he never slackened in his obedience by asking the prior to excuse him a task or let him do something else, but strove in the constancy of charity to fulfill every order, and with an eagerness of spirit

> greater than his bodily strength he longed to do more
> than he could. And with it he displayed such deftness
> than even the slack and negligent, when they saw him,
> were stirred to endure the sweat of honest toil. Weak
> though he was in body, his splendid spirit carried
> him through the labors of stronger and strenuous men.
> He did not spare the soft skin of his hands, but manfully
> wielded with his slender fingers the rough tools of his
> field-tasks to the admiration of all. His masters were
> frequently moved by compassion at the sight...[17]

In 1142, Abbot William of Rievaulx accorded Aelred the singular honor of sending him as his representative to Pope Innocent II in Rome. The Cistercians suspected that the archbishopric of York was being sold to King Stephen's nephew William for money and were determined to protest this case of simony.

Although Aelred does not allude to this journey in his books, historical research by Aelredian scholars[18] indicates that it was during this journey that Aelred first met Bernard and that the famous abbot of Clairvaux was impressed by the endearing personality, "the spiritual depth and the literary promise of the young monk from the distant North."[19]

The following year, 1143, Aelred was appointed novice-master at Rievaulx. The notes that Aelred kept on wax tablets to refresh his own memory and to instruct the novices, provided the foundation for his first book - <u>Mirror of Charity</u> (<u>Speculum Caritatis</u>). The title and the preface of this book were given by Bernard of Clairvaux who first requested, and then commanded Aelred to write this book.

In 1144, Aelred was appointed the abbot of the newly -

founded Cistercian abbey at Revesby. Under his leadership, the abbey prospered both materially and spiritually. In addition to his administrative and ecclesiastical duties, Aelred wrote and delivered many sermons during this period (1144-1147).

In 1147 Aelred was elected the abbot of Rievaulx and retained this position until his demise in 1167.

Aelred led an extremely active life.[20] Not only was he required to attend every September, the general chapter meeting in Citeaux, France, but he also had to visit, each year, the five Cistercian "branches" of Rievaulx. These "daughter houses" were Woburn, Revesby, Rufford, Melrose and Dundrennan. Furthermore, ecclesiastical etiquette necessitated an annual visit to Clairvaux - since Rievaulx was an "off-shoot" of that abbey.

Knowles states that

These regular appearances of such a distinguished man as Ailred, the intimate friend of the King of Scotland, at the centres of life along the great roads, must have served as an incitement to many to make use of his counsel or his eloquence, and he became more and more a public figure, one of the most considerable in the north of England.[21]

Aelred's ability to arbitrate with justice and compassion was widely known and admired and there were frequent demands on his time by a cross-section of institutions and individuals. Aelred also maintained an active and extensive correspondence[22] (which was definitely extant in the fifteenth century and was unfortunately destroyed in the turmoils of the sixteenth century) with "the pope, the kings of France, England, Scotland, most of the bishops, and magnates such as the earl of Leicester."[23] Anonymous monks and lay people were also, of course, recipients of his constant compassion.

Under Aelred's guidance, Rievaulx became a flourishing abbey. At the time of his death in 1167, there were over 140 monks and 500 lay men in Rievaulx.[24] Aelred's concept of the rôle of Rievaulx has been preserved (in his own words), thanks to the faithful chronicling of Walter Daniel. Daniel wrote:

> Ailred would say, "...Remember that 'we are sojourners as were all our fathers,' and that it is the singular and supreme glory of the house of Rievaulx that above all else it teaches tolerance of the infirm and compassion with others in their necessities...All...whether weak or strong should find in Rievaulx a haunt of peace, and there, like the fish in the broad seas, possess the welcome, happy, spacious peace of charity...There are the tribes of the strong and tribes of the weak. The house which holds toleration from the weak is not to be regarded as a house of religion. 'Thine eyes have seen me, yet being imperfect, and in Thy book all shall be written.'"[25]

During the last decade of his life (c. 1157-1167) when his body was severely racked by chronic ailments, certain dispensations were extended to Aelred by the general chapter of abbots at Citeaux.[26] However, Aelred continued his ministry without any diminution of enthusiasm. Whenever possible he travelled to various Cistercian foundations for abbatial visits, took "full part in all community duties...and never failed to carry out effectively the administration of his house."[27]

A prolific author,[28] he continued his literary activities in spite of his ill health. Even his "mausoleum", a cell which was built for Aelred near the infirmary became a gracious *salon* for sprightly dialogue between the affectionate abbot of Rievaulx and his many "sons". Walter Daniel informs us that

> The construction of this cot was, indeed, a great source of consolation to the brethren, for every day they came to it and sat in it, twenty or thirty at a time, to talk together of the spiritual delights of the Scriptures and of the observance of the Order... I lived under his rule for seventeen years, and in all that time he, merciful as he was...did not expel a single monk.[29]

Aelred died, as he had lived, prayerfully, patiently, in an ambiance of reciprocal affection. Until a few days before his death, Aelred attended religious services, delivered a sermon, spoke words of counsel and comfort to strengthen and inspire the men whom he had led and served for two decades. Walter Daniel has left us a vivid description of Aelred's end:

> For three days life lingered with slow gasps of breath. So strong was the spirit in his fragile body that, even though his body failed, he was scarce able to give way to death...To rejoice with the father, to grieve with the father, was an act of piety, just as it is the part of a son to bewail the death of a father and also, as he is still a father, to rejoice with him in his happy release...[30]

> ...Until the end his five senses were unimpaired, but the words which he spoke were very brief...All of us came together in one, not doubting the father's passing to God, and vying with each other in pious zeal in ministering to his needs in his weakness. There were now twelve, now twenty, now forty, now even a hundred monks about him; so vehemently was this lover of us all loved by us. Blessed is that abbot who deserves so to be loved by his own. And he indeed, whose memory

is blessed for ever more, himself counted this the greatest of all blessings, that he should be chosen by God and men to be so well beloved.[31]

My God! He did not die 'in darkness, as those that have long been dead,' not so, Lord, but in Thy light, for in His light we see Thy light.[32]

Notes to CHAPTER IV

1. See A. Squire, Aelred of Rievaulx - A Study, pp. 3-12.

2. Ibid., pp. 12-15, pp. 82-86. Also see Powicke's introduction to Vita Ailredi, pp. xli-xlvii.

   See David Knowles', The Monastic Order in England, pp. 241-242.

3. A. Squire, Aelred of Rievaulx..., p. 13.

4. See Powicke's introduction to Vita Ailredi, p. xxxix.

5. Ibid., pp. xl-xli.

6. See A. Squire, Aelred of Rievaulx..., pp. 12, 81
   Also see A. Lang's A History of Scotland, Vol. I, pp. 106-8.

7. See Powicke's introduction to Vita Ailredi, pp. lxxi-lxxv. Also see Squire's Aelred of Rievaulx..., pp. 12-13, 15-17, 19, 23, 27, 65, 99.

8. A. Squire, Aelred of Rievaulx..., pp. 13-14.

9. Ibid., pp. 3-4.

10. Walter Daniel, Vita Ailredi, pp. 3-4.

11. Aelred, Mirror of Charity I: 79: "Et dicebant homines, attendentes quaedam circa me, sed nescientes quid ageretur in me: O quam bene ist illi! O quam bene est illi! Ignorabant enim, quia ibi mihi male erat, ubi solum poterat bene esse. Valde enim intus erat plaga

mea, crucians, terrens, et intolerabili fetore omnia interiora mea corrumpens; et nisi cito admouisses manum, non tolerans meipsum, forte pessimum desperationis remedium adhibuissem."

12. See Powicke's introduction to *Vita Ailredi*, pp. xliii-xliv.

13. A. Squire, *Aelred of Rievaulx...*, p. 19.

14. Walter Daniel, *Vita Ailredi*, p. 14.

15. *Ibid.*, p. 15.

16. A. Squire, *Aelred of Rievaulx...*, pp. 19-22.

17. Walter Daniel, *Vita Ailredi*, p. 22.

18. See A. Squire, *Aelred of Rievaulx...*, pp. 23, 25.

    See Powicke's introduction to *Vita Ailredi*, pp. lvii-lix.

19. See Douglas Roby's introduction to Aelred's *Spiritual Friendship*, p. 9.

20. See David Knowles, *The Monastic Order in England*, pp. 262-266.

    See Douglas Roby's article entitled "Chimaera of the North: The Active Life of Aelred of Rievaulx" in *Cistercian Ideals and Reality*, ed. by John R. Sommerfeldt (Kalamazoo, Michigan: Cistercian Publications, 1978), pp. 152-169.

    See Powicke's introduction to *Vita Ailredi*, pp. lxiii-lxiv.

21. David Knowles, *The Monastic Order in England*, p. 263.

22. Walter Daniel, *Vita Ailredi*, p. 42.

23. David Knowles, *The Monastic Order in England*, p. 264.
    See Douglas Roby, "Chimaera of the North...", p. 152.

24. See Powicke's introduction to *Vita Ailredi*, lxiv.
    See Walter Daniel, "Epistola ad Mauricium," p. 79.

25. Walter Daniel, *Vita Ailredi*, pp. 37-38.

26. *Ibid.*, p. 39.

27. David Knowles, *The Monastic Order in England*, p. 265.

28. Powicke's list, though not definitive, is well-researched and helpful. See Powicke's "Notes on Aelred's Writings", p. xcvii:

1143-3	Speculum Caritatis
1153-4	Genealogia regum Anglorum
1153-7	Tractatus de Jesu puero duodenni
1154-60	Life of St. Ninian
1155-7	Tract on the battle of the Standard
c. 1158-63	Homilies super onus Babilonis in Ysaia, published 1163-4.
c. 1158-65	De sanctimoniali de Watton
c. 1160	De spirituali amicitia
c. 1160-2	De institutione inclusarum
1162-3	Life of Edward the Confessor
1163	Exposition, in honour of St. Edward, of the gospel lesson, Nemo accendit lucernam
1165-6	De anima

29. Walter Daniel informs us that during the last ten years (1157-1167) of Aelred's life when his body was constantly racked by physical ailments, he lived in a cell which adjoined the infirmary and conducted his duties from there. See W. Daniel, *Vita Ailredi*, pp. 41-42:

"In that abode of his he wrote many memorable works. Indeed, before this period he published a life of David, King of Scotland, in the form of a lamentation, and added to it a genealogy of King of England, the younger Henry. Also, before that, he sent to Ivo, a monk of Wardon, out of the library of his heart, a noble exposition of the lesson in the gospel beginning 'When Jesus was twelve years old,' a brilliant treatment of the threefold meaning, historical, moral and mystical. But it was in that private closet that he wrote and finished with his own hand the thirty-three homilies on the burden of Babylon, in Isaiah,[3] and, after these, other fine and profitable works. Later, he published in three books the dialogue on spiritual friendship. In the first of these he introduced the aforesaid Ivo as the questioner and joined me with himself in the subsequent discussion. And after these he wrote a book to his sister, the chaste virgin who was a recluse, in which he traced the course of this kind of profession from the ardour of the entrance into the same to its perfection. This done, he published the life of the most holy King Edward, a work whose pages shine with the great glory and splendour of the miracles. Next he expounded in honour of the same saint and to be read with the passage at his solemn vigils the gospel lesson which begins, 'No man, when he hath lighted a candle, putteth it under a bushel but on a candlestick.' He wrote this at the request of his kinsman Laurence, the Abbot of Westminster, and to please the brethren there serving God. After which he finished two books of his work about the soul, that is, its nature, extent and quality, and other matters relating to the soul, and he almost finished the third book, but his end in this life came before he brought it to a close. He paid the debt of all flesh before he had finished it. Throughout the course of this literary activity (inter hec) he was sending letters to the lord Pope, to the King of France, the King of England, the King of Scotland, the Archbishops of Canterbury and York and nearly every bishop in England, also to the most distinguished men in the Kingdom of England and especially to the Earl of Leicester, letters written with a noble pen to every grade of the ecclesiastical order, in which he left a living image of himself, for what he there commended in writing he himself practised in life, and lived much better than he could say. Unless I am wrong, he preached about two hundred most eloquent sermons, worthy of all praise, in our chapters, in synods and to the people."

30. Ibid., p. 40.

31. Ibid., pp. 60-61

32. Ibid., p. 59.

33. Ibid., p. 63.

CHAPTER V

SOME REFLECTIONS ON WALTER DANIEL'S
VITA AILREDI

Neither his contemporaries[1] nor posterity[2] have been particularly kind to Walter Daniel, the earliest biographer of Aelred of Rievaulx. Abbot Aelred himself has left us a vivid vignette of his irascible "son" Walter in the second part of Spiritual Friendship (De Spirituali Amicitia).[3] Walter Daniel's impatience with the fact that Aelred's administrative duties necessitated conversation with government officials and his (i.e. Walter Daniel's) consequent anger, did not escape the affectionate but amused observation[4] of the abbot of Rievaulx.

Moreover, Walter Daniel's biography of Aelred of Rievaulx (with whom he was closely acquainted for seventeen years) was severely criticized by two of his co-religionists.[5] These two "prelates" accused Walter Daniel of a fertile imagination. They doubted whether any of the miracles that

Daniel attributed to Aelred had actually occurred and they cited self-condemnatory passages[6] in Aelred's own works to refute Daniel's description of the "purity" of Aelred's pre-monastic life.

Consequently, Walter Daniel felt compelled to write a lengthy letter to Abbot Maurice. This letter was prefixed to the Vita Ailredi and served as its introduction. In this epistle Walter Daniel vigorously attempted to refute the charge of untruthfulness levied against him by the "two prelates," by citing the names of various living witnesses[7] and alibis who could corroborate his statements in the Vita Ailredi. Moreover, with an ingenious, perhaps casuistic, use of synecdoche Walter Daniel tried to indicate that he had not been dishonest in his depiction of Aelred's pre-monastic life - his early youth in the court of King David I of Scotland.

> I did not refer to the darnel but called attention to the wheat. I kept silence about the vices and insinuated the virtues. When, I beg, is corn without husks? No one is free from stain, not even the infant a day old. There is a rhetorical figure called in-tellectio, by which the whole is known from a small part or a part from the whole. When I applied the word 'monk' to Ailred, I was making use of this figure, attributing a part by means of the whole, calling him a monk not because he was completely chaste but because he was truly humble. Humility and chastity make the proper monk, and since a good monk never lacks humility and the whole is known from a small part and the rule of speech is not infringed but laudably observed in this mode of expression, I said well when I used the word 'monk' to describe a humble man. Those friends of mine, therefore have unjustly abused me.[8]

In spite of the title (<u>Vita Ailredi</u>) of his book, Walter Daniel's intention, was to write a hagiography, not a biography. As a medieval monk, he was following a long established tradition and drew on "the early fifth-century life of St. Martin by Sulpicius Severus,"[9] a literary debt which he acknowledged in his letter to Abbot Maurice.[10] Daniel's chronicle of diverse miracles, all attributed to the departed Aelred, seem to be a consequence of his hagiographical intention. Professor Powicke's comments, though somewhat lengthy, are worth quoting in this context:

> The <u>Vita Ailredi</u> was written to prove Ailred's claim to sanctity. It is a piece of hagiography. From Walter Daniel's point of view the external incidents of the abbot's life were important just so far as they helped to establish his case. Inevitably he saw and heard from others the things which the friend and biographer of a saint would expect to see or hear. A supernatural light shone round the infant's head; the child uttered prophecies; the youth was virtuous; the monk possessed miraculous powers of healing, which could be transmitted by his staff; he saw prophetic visions; the elements favored him, as when the rain spared his bed in the leaky house at Dundrennan; he was rigidly ascetical, stern to himself, while gracious and forgiving to others; his death was exemplary and, in spite of his age and intense physical sufferings, his corpse was as fresh and white as that of a little child.
>
> As a contribution to the hagiographical literature of the twelfth century Walter's work has no special interest or originality. The repetition of familiar precedents from the Gospels is the basis of the narrative; and parallels to most of the extravagant additions can be found in any other work of the period, for example, in the miracles of St. John of Beverley, St. Cuthbert, St. Ninian, St. Kentigern, or - to take Ailred's contemporaries - in the Lives of Godric of Finchale, William of York, Waldef of Melrose. The Latin Life of St. Modwenna, compiled in Ailred's youth by Geoffrey, abbot of Burton-on-Trent, and the basis of the later poetical Life in Anglo-French, illustrates this very well...

Walter Daniel adopted phrases in current use, just as the chroniclers used forms and phrases handed down from Levy or Sallust to adorn a speech or describe a military raid. We must not conclude that the occasions of Ailred's miracles were invented. No one would argue that, because other saints stood up to their necks in cold water in order to expel the lusts of the flesh, the story that Ailred did the same is an invention; and it would be equally hazardous to argue that Ailred's personality had no therapeutic influence, because his cures are described in the high-flown conventional language used in other lives of saints...But at this point the historian is brought to a stand. He cannot estimate the ratio between the varying degrees of suggestion or hallucination, of folk-lore or falsehood. He can only call attention to the spiritual circumstances in which a monk of the twelfth century lived. Walter Daniel and his companions breathed an atmosphere in which they could hardly escape far-fetched...interpretations of the evidence of their senses...

There would be no limits, save those imposed by the conventions of contemporary literature, to the conclusions which these eagerly expectant admirers of Ailred would draw from the most trivial incident... Prepared to see everywhere traces of the direct intervention of God, their senses were deadened to the commonplace and unusually aware of strange or peculiar circumstance. A presentiment, a coincidence, a flicker of sunlight in an unusual place, might suggest a miracle for which there were a dozen parallels. They would nudge each other with significant looks, and as they talked it over would invest the original incident with its setting of appropriate detail. The story would be complete, the witnesses ready, within an hour."

However, it is important to note that Walter Daniel's ultimate emphasis is consistently on Aelred's charity, not on supernatural events. He assures Abbot Maurice in his epistle to him:

> ...I marvel at the charity of Ailred more than I should marvel if he had raised four men from the dead. My hearers may laugh, they may mock at my words, they may throw my letter in the fire, they may do as they please, I hold fast and hope I may hold fast to this, that Ailred's charity, 'out of a pure heart, and of a good conscience and of faith unfeigned,' exceeded every novelty of miracle.[12]

In spite of the morass of medieval hagiographical material in the Vita Ailredi, there are vivid vignettes in it of the humanism, humor and persuasive caritas of the Aelred with whom a careful reader of his works is inevitably, closely acquainted. At times Walter Daniel (who was probably the infirmarian of Rievaulx) desists from what Professor Powicke termed his penchant for "pathological extravaganza." Instead of constantly chronicling physical and mental maladies and their cure by his abbot, Walter Daniel sometimes records the actual words and actions of Aelred of Rievaulx. Aelred's words, describing the rôle of Rievaulx. (quoted in the previous chapter)[13] were preserved by Walter Daniel, as well as descriptions of Aelred's cheerful fortitude during his final illness.

However, it would be incorrect to assume that Aelred's cross was confined to physical suffering, evoked and enhanced by the ascetical excesses of this otherwise moderate and modest humanist. Walter Daniel informs us that Aelred's life, from youth to (premature) age, was never free from the presence of a handful of detractors. As a favored youth in the court of King David I of Scotland, Aelred was once severely maligned by a disgruntled courtier[14] whom he subsequently won as a friend. Although Aelred's election as the abbot of Rievaulx in 1147, evoked general acclaim, certain dissatisfied co-religionists[15] accused him of ambition.

Moreover, these detractors[16] were unsympathetic when acute arthritis and other ailments forced Aelred, during the last decade of his life, to slightly modify his demanding schedule as abbot, author, arbitrator of disputes and advisor to a cross-section of people (kings, popes, magnates, unknown monks and laity - all had access to his affection and advice). Walter Daniel also informs us in his <u>Vita Ailredi</u> and in "Epistola ad Mauricium" that, in spite of Aelred's persistent <u>caritas</u> and pastoral loyalty to his flock, several of his monks caused him anguish and anxiety and one demented man actually tried to murder him.[17]

Gandhi had once observed that "The art of dying follows as a corollary to the art of living."[18]

Dedication to his vocation and a serene acceptance of its varied demands had marked the life of Aelred. Confronted with deranged brawn, Aelred faced his would-be assassin with his characteristic composure and compassion. In his letter to Abbot Maurice, Walter Daniel has left for posterity a vivid description of that surprising scene.

> And, as we (Ailred and Walter) sat alone...behold a monk entered, mad with rage...He came to where Ailred lay. Bellowing cruelly and gnashing his teeth he seized hold of a side of the mat, with the father lying on it, tossed them both up with all his might, and hurled the father of at least a hundred monks and five hundred laymen into the fire among the cinders, shouting "O, you wretch, now I am going to kill you, now I am going to destroy you by a hard death. What are you doing, lying here, you imposter, you useless, silly fellow? You shall tell no more of your lies, for now you are about to die.' I was consumed by the sight, and not

suffering the danger to the father, rose in hot indignation against the bully and, eager to turn the tables on him once and for all, took him hard by the beard...In the meantime some of the monks appeared and found the man, like a wolf standing over a sheep, or rather, the shepherd, straining to get at him to tear him with his teeth and devour him in his cruel jaws. They also were consumed by what they saw and, in their burning zeal, would have laid their hands upon the son of pestilence, had not the father, heedless of his infirmity and mindful only of the call of charity, bade them desist: 'No, no, I beg; no, my sons...I am quite all right, I am not hurt, I am not upset; this son of mine who threw me into the fire, has cleansed, not destroyed me. He is my son, but he is ill. I am indeed not sound of body, but he in his sickness has made me sound in soul, for blessed are the peacemakers, for they shall be called the sons of God.' And then, taking his head in his hands, the most blessed man kisses him, blesses and embraces him, and gently sought to soothe his senseless anger against himself, just as though he himself felt no pain from his own sickness and had been touched by no sadness because of the injury done to him. Oh, the charity of the man, greater than many miracles. He did not order him to be expelled from the monastery, or beaten or bound or fettered as a madman; he would not suffer anybody to reproach him with a chiding word. 'It was,' he said, 'against my person that he sinned, and I, when I wish, will revenge myself, but I never shall...'[19]

Although Aelred was not killed by the hand of this malevolent monk but died due to natural causes, one is, again, anachronistically reminded by Aelred's *caritas* of Mahatma Gandhi's prophetic words about his own end and the strength and dignity with which he died. Shortly before he was assassinated Gandhi had said:

Have I that nonviolence of the brave in me? My death alone will show that. If someone killed me and I died with a prayer for the assassin on my lips, and God's remembrance and consciousness of His living presence in the sanctuary of my heart, then alone would I be said to have had the nonviolence of the brave.[20]

Aelred's final days were lived, as was his life, in a tenor of unbroken prayer, and whenever possible, service to others. He labored for his men as long as he could and when he was seized by the final grip of illness, the fortitude and fervor of his prayerful end continued to be a source of friendly inspiration to his grieving "sons".[21]

Aelred Squire concedes that

> Walter's Life gives us a framework and a rough chronology into which to fit the output of Aelred's career as a writer.[22]

However, it is not unreasonable to assert that the Vita Ailredi does more than provide us with a "rough chronology" into which one can fit the corpus of Aelred's works.

Many anecdotes and asides intimately related to Aelred's life would have been lost without the faithful chronicling of Walter Daniel. Daniel recorded in detail the circumstances which led to Aelred's entry[23] into Rievaulx, as well as anecdotes about his childhood, boyhood and youth[24] which he heard from Aelred's father, from the aged monk Simon,[25] Abbot of Sartis (who was the novice-master of Rievaulx during Aelred's novitiate), from monks[26] who were under Aelred's care and from Aelred himself.[27]

In spite of Walter Daniel's distaste for the administrative duties which even Cistercian abbots had to perform, he has given us some valuable glimpses of Aelred's public life. Thanks to Walter Daniel, we know that Aelred was sent to Rome in 1142[28] by Abbot William of Rievaulx, to express the Cistercians' objection to the election of William, King Stephen's kinsman, to the archbishopric of York. Walter Daniel informs us that Aelred's mission to Pope Innocent II was successful.

> When the Abbot (i.e. William of Rievaulx) sent him to Rome on the famous case of the dissension at York he was received so graciously by the Lord Pope, and expounded the business and brought it to a conclusion with such energy, that the esteem and admiration which he won after his return were widespread. It was then that the lord William put him in charge of the novices...[29]

Walter Daniel has also preserved for posterity some other salient facts about the ministry of Aelred of Rievaulx. He informs us about Aelred's arbitration in Galloway, and his reconciliation of a warring, northern king and his sons,[30] Daniel also refers to Aelred's visits (in spite of grave physical illness) to the "daughter houses" of Rievaulx.[31] Aelred was in Scotland, a year before his death, in 1166, and in Dundrennan Abbey (believed to have been founded by his former patron, King David I) in 1163.[32]

Daniel refers to Aelred's earliest work, the <u>Mirror of Charity</u>[33] and mentions the books[34] which Aelred wrote during the last decade of his life. Thanks to Daniel, we know with certainty that Aelred's gracious dialogue[35] on <u>Spiritual Friendship</u> (<u>De Spirituali Amicitia</u>) was penned when he was racked by physical pain - although the unruffled tenor of this book does not give us a hint of this fact. Daniel also informs us about the large correspondence (extant until the sixteenth century) that Aelred maintained, in spite of his ill health, and the sermons which he wrote and delivered.

> Throughout the course of this literary activity...
> he was sending letters to the lord Pope, to the King
> of France, the King of England, the King of Scotland,
> the Archbishops of Canterbury and York and nearly every
> bishop in England, also to the most distinguished men
> in the Kingdom of England and especially to the Earl
> of Leicester, letters written with a noble pen to every
> grace of the ecclesiastical order, in which he left a
> living image of himself, for what he there commended
> in writing he himself practised in life, and lived
> much better than he could say. Unless I am wrong, he
> preached about two hundred most eloquent sermons,
> worthy of all praise, in our chapters, in synods and
> to the people.[36]

Walter Daniel is also the source which informs us that Aelred's last work, On the Soul (De Anima), was left unfinished when he died in 1167.[37]

The lengthy descriptions of miracles which Daniel attributes to Aelred of Rievaulx not only strain the credulity of "modern" readers but raised the eyebrows of some of his own contemporaries and co-religionists as well. However, in spite of its cargo of hagiographical material, Walter Daniel's Vita Aelredi continues to be a seminal work for anyone who is interested in Aelred of Rievaulx. This was the first book that was written about Aelred and, in spite of his lack of objectivity, the author had the advantage of close acquaintance with the abbot of Rievaulx for seventeen years. Consequently, Daniel did make an important contribution to Aelredian scholarship.

Interest in Aelred of Rievaulx and his works almost died out about a hundred years after his demise. The catholic contribution of the remarkable humanist was viewed with suspicion in the late Middle Ages when the twelfth century's optimistic view of human potentiality and dignity was replaced by a somewhat sombre mood. The dissolution of the English monasteries during the reign of Henry VIII in the sixteenth century, caused the loss of Aelred's letters and[38] the dispersion of his works. The increasingly secular tone and tenor of Tudor England was, of course, not conducive to continuity of interest in Britain's Anglo-Saxon, Catholic heritage.

It was not until the nineteenth century that a highly romanticized interest in her medieval heritage reawakened in literary circles in England. Professor F. M. Powicke who was born in Victorian England was not immune to the current of interest in the Middle Ages which was prevalent in his day. He became a distinguished medievalist and an Oxford don and contributed substantially to his field. Thanks to Professor Powicke whose <u>Aelred of Rievaulx and his Biographer</u> appeared in 1922 and whose critical edition of the <u>Vita Ailredi</u> is invaluable in the realm of Aelredian scholarship, a serious interest in Aelred of Rievaulx was kindled in the twentieth century among medievalists, historians, humanists, scholars, clerics and theologians. This distinguished group includes David Knowles, A. Squire, Amédée Hallier, R. W. Southern, Louis Bouyer, Adele Fiske, Douglas Roby, Marie Anne Mayeski, Thomas Merton and John R. Sommerfeldt

Notes to CHAPTER V

1. See Walter Daniel, "Epistola ad Mauricium", pp. 1, 78, 79.

2. See A. Squire, *Aelred of Rievaulx*..., pp. 1-2.

3. See Aelred's *Spiritual Friendship*, pp. 69-87.

4. *Ibid.*, p. 69.

5. See Walter Daniel, "Epistola ad Mauricium", p. 1

6. Aelred, *Mirror of Charity* I: 79. (See n. 11, Chapter IV of this dissertation).

    Also see Aelred, "Rule of Life for a Recluse" in *Treatise and Pastoral Prayer* (2nd ed.; Kalamazoo, Michigan: Cistercian Publications, 1982), pp. 93-96.

7. See Walter Daniel, "Epistola ad Mauricium", pp. 67-69.

8. *Ibid.*, p. 76.

9. See A. Squire, *Aelred of Rievaulx*..., p. 1.

10. *Ibid.*, p. 2.

11. See Powicke's introduction to Walter Daniel's *Vita Ailredi*, pp. lxxvi-lxxviii.

12. Walter Daniel, "Epistola ad Mauricium", p. 78.

13. See p. 33, Chapter IV.

14. See Walter Daniel's *Vita Ailredi*, pp. 6-8.

15. *Ibid.*, p. 33.

16. *Ibid.*, p. 34.

17. Walter Daniel, "Epistola ad Mauricium", p. 79.

18. Quoted by Eknath Easwaran in *Gandhi the Man* (San Francisco: Glide Publications, 1973), p. 140.

19. Walter Daniel, "Epistola ad Mauricium", pp. 79-80.

20. Quoted by Eknath Easwaran in *Gandhi the Man*, p. 101.

21. See *Vita Ailredi*, pp. 55-62.

22. A. Squire, *Aelred of Rievaulx...*, p. 2.

23. See *Vita Ailredi*, pp. 14-15.

24. Walter Daniel, "Epistola ad Mauricium", pp. 71-73.

25. See *Vita Ailredi*, pp. 16-17.

26. *Ibid.*, p. 23.

27. *Ibid.*, pp. 27, 37, 43, 48, 52, 57-58.

28. *Ibid.*, p. 23.

29. *Ibid.*

30. *Ibid.*, 45-46.

31. Walter Daniel, "Epistola ad Mauricium", pp. 74-75.

32. See Powicke's notes - numbers one and four - in *Vita Ailredi*, p. 45.

33. See *Vita Ailredi*, pp. 25-26.

34. *Ibid.*, pp. 41-42.

35. See David Knowles' comment (on *Spiritual Friendship*) in *The Monastic Order in England*, p. 262: "The writer an infirm, tireless abbot, the ruler of a vast household, the counsellor of bishops and kings, who snatched time, between his solitary prayer and the visits of those who needed his help, to add a few sentences to the roll in his bare and comfortless cell."

    Also note Squire's observations in *Aelred of Rievaulx...*, pp. 100-101.

36. *Vita Ailredi*, p. 42.

37. *Ibid.*

38. Douglas Roby, "Chimaera of the North..." in *Cistercian Ideals and Reality*, p. 152.

CHAPTER VI

MIRROR OF CHARITY

(SPECULUM CARITATIS)

Aelred's Mirror of Charity was written at the insistence of Bernard of Clairvaux whom he had met in 1142 on his (i.e. Aelred's) journey to Rome. Aelred had initially parried Bernard's request, claiming to lack scholarship, as well as spiritual refinement. Professor Powicke has aptly observed that

> The abbot of Clairvaux brushed his excuses aside. Taking up Aelred's plea that he was almost illiterate and had come from the kitchens, not from the schools, he made characteristic play with it, in a series of phrases culled from the Scriptures. That Ailred is no grammarian fans rather than puts out the spark of Bernard's desire...He (Ailred) had spoken of his rough and hard retreat, among rocks and hills, where he works with axe and hammer under a rule of silence; but, Bernard replies,
>
>> "I find no terror either in the hard mountain steeps, nor in the rough rocks nor in the hollow places of the valleys...Wherefore I judge that with that hammer of yours you may cut out those rocks that you would not find by your native sagacity in the

> libraries of the professors, and that not seldom, in the midday heat, you will be aware, under the shade of the trees, of something that you would never have learned in the schools..."[1]

> "In Christ's name and by the Spirit of our God do I command you to write down without delay what your own meditations have taught you about the excellence of charity, the fruits of charity and everything that charity involves. Thus, as in a mirror, others may come to understand what charity is, how its possession brings delight, and how its contrary vice, cupidity, imposes nothing but tyranny. Your book will show how false it is to think that charity is lessened by a life of austerity, and that in fact austerity increases charity. It will tell us also how charity must be exercised and manifested in our conduct. And because you feel so embarrassed about writing the book, you can put this letter of mine as a preface to it, so that if anyone is not pleased with what you have written in your _Mirror of Charity_ (that is the title I wish the book to have), he can blame me, for having forced you to write against your will, instead of you, who did the work under obedience."[2]

In deference to Bernard's insistence, Aelred agreed to accept this task which he completed in a surprisingly short time - a few months. This fact led Squire, one of the chief Aelredian scholars of our time, to posit the theory that Aelred's _Mirror of Charity_ was compiled from his extensive extant notes, jotted down during his tenure as a novice-master.

One of the compelling characteristics of Aelred's _Mirror of Charity_ is its dialectical quality. His intense interest in and love for the Hebrew scriptures was at odds with prevalent medieval "Christian" concepts about Jews. His advocacy of the inclusiveness of _caritas_ - love of enemies and of incompatible people, is juxtaposed to his innate appreciation of of the joys of friendship with a few like-minded companions. Moreover, his own extremely ascetical tendencies and his rational applause of the classical concepts of moderation and balance, pose another interesting contrast. His love of classical humanism and his Christian asceticism, his praise of monasticism and his exposé of its malpractitioners, his persistent interest in pre-Christian Latin literature and his desire to extol the uniqueness of the Bible - all jostle for attention in the Mirror of Charity and are ultimately brought into some degree of synthesis by Aelred of Rievaulx.

In spite of his ability to be allegorical and discursive, Aelred could also be pithy. He tells us

> Charity - a short word indeed, but with its meaning of perfect and unalloyed love, it sums up the whole of man's attitude to God and His creatures.[3]

In an attempt to incorporate some of the ideas and ideals of the Hebrew Bible, Aelred included in the Mirror of Charity his own interpretations of the rite of circumcision[4] and the meaning of the sabbath[5] - both of which he regarded as concepts crucial to the practice of charity.

In the third section of his Mirror of Charity, Aelred continues at some length his reflections on and interpretations of the three kinds of sabbaths. As mentioned earlier, in spite of his medieval tendency to be lengthily allegorical and discursive, Aelred was able to succinctly summarize his concepts.

Aelred wrote:

> In each Sabbath we find rest and peace and joy for the spirit, but the first belongs to a man's own quiet conscience, the second to a community of men living happily together, and the third consists in contemplation of God. The first Sabbath is rest from sin, the second is rest from cupidity and the third we see Him as He is in Himself, as God. First we are recollected in our own soul, then we are drawn to the love of our fellow men, and finally we are lifted up to heaven.[6]

Aelred's intrinsically affective temperament naturally inclined him towards love of kin and friends. Although he was honor-bound in his rôle as a monastic author to warn his readers against the dangers of nepotism[7] and partiality, he nevertheless draws upon the Hebrew Bible to emphasize the positive aspects of "natural loves." He tells us that

> The love of one's own family we find among the holiest of men, as for instance the patriarchs of the Old Testament...[8]

In the realm of friendship, Aelred regarded the fraternal love of Jonathan for David as a paradigm of _philia_ - a relationship in which unselfish idealism is nurtured and balanced by reason, altruism and loyalty to the highest ideals of friendship:

> These various conflicting feelings in the soul raise the problem of how they shall be properly ordered and organized. We must consider which is to be preferred to another, and how the better may be given place over what is less good...Jonathan...instead of acquiescing to his own father's plan to kill David, followed the dictates of reasonable love for his virtuous friend... Only Jonathan, do we read, put his father, the king, and the country of his inheritance at less value than his great friend David. He could rightly have said: 'I will be king and thou shalt be second after me.' If he had done this it would have been no violation of the laws of friendship...Jonathan was bound to his

father by a son's obligations, but to David he was bound by feelings of love and friendship...he owed a friend's love to David and his pledge could not be broken.[9]

Aelred's medieval love of "proper order," both internal and societal, led him to apply a hierarchical norm to the "reasonable ordering" of the affections. Again, he turned to the Hebrew Bible for a vivid symbol to express his convictions. Aelred tells us:

> Let us imagine our heart to be a kind of spiritual Noah's Ark, made of the imperishable wood of virtues and good deeds. There we shall find various compartments on different levels made ready for the different kinds of people we shall meet.[10]

In spite of his strong attraction to the Hebrew Bible, unfortunately Aelred's <u>Mirror of Charity</u> does contain some traces of the author's misunderstanding of some Jewish customs.[11] However, his ascetical impatience of rituals and aesthetic expressions of devotion are not confined to his misconception of some Jewish practices but are directed, with greater severity, to his co-religionists.[12] In spite of Aelred's belief in the prevalent Christian notion that spiritual salvation was possible only if one embraced Christianity, there is no evidence in his life and works (or in contemporary accounts about him) that Aelred was ever guilty of hostile acts towards non-Christians - or any person for that matter! Unlike Bernard of Clairvaux, his religious superior, Aelred refused to advocate militant action against anyone (the most obvious medieval targets being heretics, Jews and Muslims). Aelred preferred to adhere to his unflinching faith in the intrinsic, ineffable goodness of God's creation:

> God's being is above all other modes of being. It cannot be communicated to anyone but God, nor can it undergo any change. It is this same God who has given to every creature its nature, its beauty and its purpose. Thus all created things are good and beautiful, and all have a fixed purpose. All this is God's doing. Everything has its being from the highest and incommunicable being. Everything derives its beauty from the supremely and incommunicably beautiful.
>
> The same is true for goodness and wisdom, and all the other qualities that creatures possess. Everything created is by its nature good, and by its form beautiful. It has for its purpose the embellishment of the whole of creation. Hence when God looked at all that He had made, He saw that it was good. A thing is good simply because it is made by God. It is composed of parts that harmonize with each other. It is ordained to fulfill a certain purpose in so far as it performs, in the plan of the universe, a function in accordance with the mode, the time and the place of its existence.
>
> Thus each thing has a place which fits its mode of existence. For example, the proper place of the angels is in heaven, and the irrational creation belongs to the earth, but man, who comes between these two realms of earth and heaven, has a paradise which is both corporeal and spiritual. As regards position and duration likewise, everything has been accounted for in God's beautiful design. The angels were all created at the same time, and they will never cease to be. Men were not all created at the same time, but they none-the-less have eternal life.[13]

Douglas Roby's comments regarding Aelred and Bernard are thought-provoking and worth remembering when contrasting these two remarkable Cistercians:

> "If he (Aelred) lacked the burning single-mindedness of Bernard, he had a warmth of love which did not scorch as Bernard's sometimes did. Bernard preached a crusade and destroyed Abelard for the sake of the love of God; Aelred preferred to reconcile enemies and write of the virtue of friendship. He was a man whose love was great enough to prove that greatness does not need to be brutal,

and that to be a saint one does not have to despise human affections."[14]

Counsel through conversation.

Aelred used the dialogue form in two later works - Spiritual Friendship (De Spirituali Amicitia) and On the Soul (De Anima). Here, in his first book, Mirror of Charity (Speculum Caritatis), he begins to explore the use of dialogue in a limited, experimental manner.

Each of the three parts of the Mirror of Charity, contains a dialogue. The first dialogue is with a fool, the second is with a novice and the third with an Augustinian canon.

In the first dialogue, Aelred queries the fool about the source, nature and recipients of wisdom. The fool insists that angels, not humans, are wise. Aelred assures him that angels do not generate wisdom but that wisdom comes from the ineffable Source. The fool, hoping to checkmate Aelred, then specifically asks him where wisdom can indeed be discovered. Aelred's cheerful rejoinder is as follows:

> You must admit, then, that wisdom exists, to be found at the end of the search by those who seek to become wise. If it did not already exist, you could not possibly find it.[15]

The fool, however, is unwilling to concede that wisdom has any other source except a secular one. He consequently contends that wisdom comes "by knowledge and by the use of our minds."

Hoping to wean him from his rigidly secular position, Aelred tries to make the fool reflect on spiritual possibilities by posing further questions to him. He asks the fool:

> You must obtain your wisdom from somewhere, and if you say that you got it from a wise man, he in turn must have got it from some other wise man. Even if we acquired wisdom from the angels, they would have had to get it from someone else first...Did you always exist then? Where did your being come from?[16]

The fool reluctantly concedes that finite reason cannot account for all mysteries. However, he prefers to place his faith on an angel, instead of God. Aelred silences this superstition by insisting that angels have no wisdom or power that is not derived from God - that angels, too, are created beings, though of an obviously greater stature than mortals. This dialogue ends with the following words by Aelred to the still stubborn fool:

> Obviously we are forced to the conclusion that <u>all</u> created beings have their being from an uncreated being, and that <u>all</u> wisdom is derived from uncreated wisdom.[17]

This dialogue between Aelred and a proponent of secular knowledge (who is termed "a fool") is followed by Aelred's reflections on the misuse of love and by the restoration of the divine image by love.

In the second part of the <u>Mirror of Charity</u>, another dialogue takes place, this time it is a conversation between Aelred and a novice. The novice was puzzled "why it was that he had received in his previous worldly condition much more spiritual consolation - both of compunction and of the extreme feeling of God's love - than he did in the monastery."[18]

Aelred's "wise direction of souls" is revealed in a series of frank, firm but non-judgmental questions that he poses to the novice. Aelred himself discloses to us his counseling method:

> I answered him by asking him a question, namely did he think that the life he had led in the world was holier and more acceptable to God than the way of life he followed in the monastery?[19]

The novice honestly states that this was not so, and adds, with a touch of humor, that his frolicking friends would have regarded him as a saint, had he lived then, as he did now. Aelred goes on to ask the novice if he had reflected on the Pauline injunction (that many tribulations have to be experienced before entering God's kingdom) or whether he had, in fact, undergone any difficulties in his pre-monastic life for the sake of Truth. The novice is forced to admit that he had never reflected on such notions nor had he performed any penances. On the contrary, he had lived entirely for his own amusement. The novice admits that in spite of his former, self-centered lifestyle, he had been "conscious of loving Christ very deeply" and he had wept at times overcome by the intensity of this love. He confesses that spiritual yearnings, however, did not stop him

> "from going straight back to my usual amusements, the company of friends and relatives, eating too much, drinking too much, sleeping late into the day, giving way to every feeling of anger or discontent, fighting, coveting other people's property, and indulging my own will in every way."[20]

In order to help the novice see in greater detail, the contrast between his past and present lifestyles, Aelred asks

him to describe his current mode of life. The novice's answer
depicts in vivid detail a factual portrait of the daily life
of the Cistercians of Rievaulx, during the twelfth century.
It was a life denuded of physical comforts or aesthetic luxuries,
requiring manual labor, mental discipline and emotional resil-
ience and, above all, the sacrifice of narcissism. "There is
no place for self-will and no time for idleness", the novice
admits. However, the youth lists some solid benefits. The
residents of the Rievaulx community were not harassed by liti-
gations nor importuned by the roving poor and enjoyed mental
peace living as they did in a tranquil and stable environment.
Moreover, unlike secular society, birth and rank did not give
a monk privileges or opportunities to "lord it over" those of
humbler parentage.

> And what I love above everything else is that there is
> no consideration of persons for the rank they held in
> the world, for birth makes no difference here. We are
> only treated differently according to our needs - if
> we are ill, for instance, or not very strong. The
> fruits of our common work are divided among all, with
> nothing extra for favorites, but only for those in need.[21]

This egalitarian aspect of the monastery delights the
novice who waxes eloquent over the virtues of Rievaulx:

> In fact I seem to find here every perfection that the
> gospel precepts contain, and everything I read in the
> teaching of the fathers and the monks of old.[22]

Aelred aptly cautions the novice not to allow himself
to be swept away into gullibility but to maintain a balanced
perspective in order to avoid future disillusionment:

> Since you are a novice...I can put all this enthusiasm down to fervor, and not to self-satisfaction! But you must be careful to remember that there is no perfection in this life that may not be cleverly aped by people who are insincere. And I don't want you to be put off by them, when you discover frauds in the religious life as you certainly will.[23]

Aelred concludes his cautionary remarks with an opposite question:

> But tell me, now that you have described the monastic life in such detail, is it to be compared with those precious tears which you wept in the world?[24]

The monk now concedes that a few, fervent tears shed amidst luxury and license can hardly be compared to his present disciplined life of altruism and prayer. However, he is still puzzled "...it is so very odd that I seemed to love God more in those days, when in fact I was much less sure of His mercy."[25]

Aelred reminds the novice of a Biblical parable in which an obedient and a negligent servant are contrasted.[26] The novice, now convinced of the clarity of his choice of vocation, asks Aelred whether the piety and tears he had experienced in his secular life were, in fact, worthless. Aelred asserts that such spiritual stirrings are useful but he warns him

> ...remember...not to judge your love for God by these passing feelings and emotions, since we may even be moved to tears by a very good performance on a stage.[27]

The novice's memory is awakened and he confides that once he had wept as copiously when reflecting on the gospels as he had on hearing Arthurian romances. With his characteristic generosity, Aelred does not gloat over this confession but hastens to reiterate to the novice that his former feelings of piety do, indeed, have some relevance to his present life:

> I mean that these things will give you some knowledge of the truth, so that you may come to know yourself and may learn not to spare your own faults. Look how often, even against their own conscience, people put forward clever and deceptive arguments which give them an excuse for hiding their own faults even from themselves...It would be far better for them to say with the psalmist: 'Have mercy on me, O Lord, for I am weak.' Such feelings and tears will, in fact, show you not that you are wonderfully holy, but that you are weak and needy.[28]

A few chapters after Aelred's record of this conversation, the dialogue continues between Aelred and the novice. Aelred explains to the young man that there are three phases of spiritual consolation:

> In the beginning of your conversion you were given the sweet feeling of God's love in order to draw you away from evil. And after that you will find that consolation comes to refresh you on your way, so that you may not be overcome by this hard life. Finally, when you have mastered the many trials and difficulties that give you trouble at the moment, you will find that great abundance of sweetness which is laid up for those that fear the Lord.[29]

Aelred also indicates to the monk that his evaluation of his own inner life was incorrect:

> You have discovered...that you loved God much less than you thought you did. I mean that it is precisely when you thought that you loved God most that you find you loved Him less. The more negligent we are of our salvation and the more our souls are weak, the more imperfect our love is, don't you agree?[30]

Aelred emphasizes the need for contrition, the importance of penance and the necessity of cooperating with grace by amending one's foibles and follies:

> For how can there be true penance if we return to our evil ways? And therefore you, who are a novice, must work out your salvation with labor and care, with mortification of the flesh, with vigils and manual work, with poor food and rough clothes, with silence and recollection. These will make an acceptable sacrifice of your whole being - both the inner and the outer man - and tears will enkindle the flame of charity that it sends up to God.[31]

The purpose of this dialogue was to explicitly fulfill Bernard of Clairvaux's injunction to Aelred:

> Your book will show how false it is to think that charity is lessened by a life of austerity, and that in fact austerity increases charity.[32]

However, Aelred's conversation with the youth is not simply a pedagogical exercise, using the literary device of a dialogue with a fictious novice, to demonstrate a maxim. As a novice-master, and then an abbot, there were many occasions when Aelred was asked to clarify and resolve the medley of doubts and dilemmas[33] that beset the novices and monks under his pastoral care. There is a note of authenticity about this dialogue (which also gives us a glimpse of Aelred's counselling methods) which makes one venture the hypothesis that this is a record of an actual dialogue rather than an imaginary conversation.

Aelred admits that the final dialogue in the Mirror of Charity (which occurs in Park III, Chapter 35) "is something in the nature of a degression...but it is still to the point of our discussion." Adhering to Bernard of Clairvaux's injunction to defend the Cistercian rule against those who inveighed against its austerities, Aelred stages a dialogue between himself and an Augustinian canon. Neither Aelred's other works nor the accounts of those who knew him nor the tone of this dialogue suggest that, in fact, an actual debate had once occurred between Aelred and an Augustinian canon. One cannot, of course, preclude this possibility. However, it may not be unreasonable to assume that Aelred decided to cast his defense of the Cistercian rule in the format of a dialogue.

Since St. Benedict (the original author of this Rule) had allowed the Rule to be relaxed in cases of ill health or general physical infirmity, the Augustinian canon argued that this Rule was not the backbone of the Cistercians' life. Aelred's rejoinder leaves no room for casuistry: "The whole purpose of our life is contained in the Rule."

In Chapter 35 of Part III, the *Mirror of Charity*, Aelred had warned abbots against unreasonable relaxations of the Rule of St. Benedict:

> ...the one who is allowed to make dispensations must so arrange things that charity be not made to suffer because of the dispensations he allows.[34]

However, Aelred does not regard the Rule as an end in itself. It is for him and his brothers only the vehicle which enables them to grow in charity. Walker's and Webb's comments are helpful in this context:

> Thus, for Aelred, there are two abuses equally to be guarded against. The first is in ignoring regulations because they do not seem to be essential to the Rule. The second is in observing them, yet making a mockery of them by not progressing in charity, which is always the fundamental aim.[35]

Dialectical Elements in Mirror of Charity

There is a tension in Aelred of Rievaulx's <u>Mirror of Charity</u> between his Christian asceticism and the optimistic humanism of the twelfth century. On the one hand, the human journey seems to him to be at best a perilous one, fraught with many hazards through hostile territory.

> Does this world's pit of death and miry clay give true excellence? Can there be perfect knowledge in a life lived under the shadow of death? What real delight can be found in this howling waste and boundless desert? There is no excellence in this world which is not set tottering by fear, no knowledge in a man who does not really know himself, no delight in the things of the flesh that does not finally render a man as carnal as any horse or mule. If your pleasure is to be found in glory or riches, you can take none of your wealth with you when death claims you, nor will your worldly glory have any power in the land of the dead.[36]

On the other hand, this Augustinian tone can be contrasted to Aelred's enthusiastic praise of the created world and man's unique rôle in the magnificent bounty of God:

> Thus all created things are good and beautiful, and all have a fixed purpose. All this is God's doing... man, who comes between these two realms of earth and heaven, has a paradise which is both corporeal and spiritual.[37]

The medieval love of "proper order",[38] of hierarchical harmony is expressed throughout the <u>Mirror of Charity</u>. Moreover, Aelred regarded redemption not merely as a theory or a possibility. He was convinced that spiritual wholeness and restoration of the <u>imago dei</u>[39] are the fruits of genuine penitence (i.e. contrition resulting in the severance of one's narcissistic patterns of action) and subsequent whole-hearted devotion to God:

> Pride corrupted the image of God in us and led us away from God, not by means of our feet but by the desires of our hearts. We return to God by following the same path, but in the other direction, by the exercise of these same desires; and humility renews in us the same image in which God created us...This renewal can only come about by fulfilling the new commandment of charity given us by our Savior, and if the mind clothes itself in charity, our corrupted memory and knowledge will be given new life and new form. How few words are needed to express the new commandment, but how much they imply - the stripping of our old selves, the renewal of our inner life, the reshaping of the divine image within us. Our power to love was poisoned by the selfishness of our desires, and stifled by lust, so that it has tended always to seek the very depths of vicious practices. But when charity floods the soul and warms away the numbness, love strives towards higher and more worthy objects. It puts aside the old ways and takes up a new life, and on flashing wings it flies to the highest and purest Goodness which is the source of its being.[40]

Although Aelred continuously emphasizes the necessity for self-discipline, prayer, vigilance against the temptations of vanity, lust, greed, various eccentricities etc., he expresses a profoundly optimistic faith in God's abiding grace and regards evil as ultimately impotent and a servant in His plan.

> We must realize that evil, although it was not created or activated by God, is made to serve a purpose in His plan. Why, indeed, should not God, who is Almighty and infinitely good, allow the existence of an evil which cannot in the slightest way interfere with His eternal designs? His omnipotence and kindness are more clearly shown when He turns evil to good effect, making purposeless things fulfill a function, and granting heaven to the sinner.[41]

Aelred's _Mirror of Charity_ reflects the fact that his preoccupation is with the cultivation, understanding, expression and "right ordering" of charity - not with "sin" and its many manifestations. As mentioned earlier, although Aelred teaches his readers many ways in which to safeguard themselves against the onslaughts of "cupidity", he refuses to attach any abiding importance to evil:

> For my part I can say that my soul has already had enough of sin without wallowing in it any further, and I can learn a valuable lesson from the sight of evil-doers whose scheming and sinning eventually recoil upon their heads. There is no reward in sin, and if anyone finds any satisfaction in evil, it is hard to think what form this satisfaction takes.
>
> There is indeed no comparison between satiety in wickedness and the hunger of charity which leads to the fulfillment of all our deepest desires, and brings us to the completest joy and delight. Even more difficult it is to imagine any shade of comparison between the blessedness to be found in heaven and the emptiness of the dubious pleasures of sin. For the more a man strives to satisfy his longings and the desires of his bodily appetites, the more he is starving himself of the food of true values. He may be the richest and most successful man in the world, but in reality he is worse off than a beggar in the gutter.[42]

Aelred reiterates, throughout the <u>Mirror of Charity</u>, his faith in the inherent goodness and grandeur of human nature and its affective qualities. He regarded "wrong" actions as the consequence of misdirected charity - the abuse of one's innately good, creative impulse and capacity for love. The following pithy definition seems to contain the essence of Aelred's concept of charity and cupidity (as expressed in various ways throughout the <u>Mirror of Charity</u>):

> Therefore, we may define charity as the good use of love, and cupidity, its opposite, as the abuse of love.[43]

In his first work, the Mirror of Charity, Aelred does not succeed in achieving a smooth synthesis between his humanism and his asceticism. The medieval humanists' love of Latin literature (a love which Aelred shared with them), and the tendency of some scholars of his time to give equal importance to pre-Christian classics and to the Bible, are strongly denounced[44] by Aelred who stressed the supremacy of scripture and demonstrated through the Mirror of Charity his own intimate acquaintance with both the Hebrew Bible and the New Testament. Aelred's intellectual attraction and mental assent to the classical principle of moderation and harmony between the body and the mind were at odds with his own highly ascetical lifestyle and his assignment (by no less a personage than the formidable Bernard of Clairvaux) to defind the strictures of the Cistercian rule in the Mirror of Charity. Moreover, Aelred's own love of friendship and rapport with those who were "cultured" and "courteous" are traits that he subjected to careful scrutiny[45] and cited as examples to warn both himself and his readers against the danger of ready assent to these inclinations, without first examining and ascertaining their relevance to one's spiritual quest.

Aelred succeeded to a great extent in adhering to the assignment which was given to him by Bernard of Clairvaux. In the course of his first book, he does indeed discuss the nature of charity, its nurture and unfoldment and the dangers of being deflected into cupidity. However, contemporary accounts[46] and Aelred's own corpus of writings indicate that his was a deeply affective nature. Aelred was more of a mystic than a theologian, a friend and an arbitrator rather than an authoritarian. He was to many people a pastoral presence, a discursive, genial, reassuring companion rather than a crisp systematizer, a formal administrator or a rigid exponent of dogmas.

It is not surprising, therefore, that certain elements of self-disclosure (both autobiographical and affective) occasionally enter the Mirror of Charity - a book ostensibly dedicated to the exposition of charity, its "proper" exercise and a defense of the Rule of St. Benedict as understood by the Cistercians.

One of the most vivid passages in the Mirror of Charity is Aelred's lament for his deceased friend, Simon.[47] Although he had both the Augustinian[48] and the Bernadine[49] models for this eulogy, his anguish is nevertheless his own, revealing the depth of his fraternal love and loss.

In spite of Aelred's warnings against the dangers of friendship and the importance of ascertaining the purity of the relationship before embarking on it, towards the end of the Mirror of Charity Aelred frankly confesses that it is impossible to enjoy equally the company of everyone.[50] Moreover, he expresses his deep appreciation of the solace and joy of spiritual friendship with a few fellow-pilgrims with whom one has a genuine rapport.

Walter Daniel, Aelred's first biographer, was criticized by some of his contemporaries and co-religionists for extolling Aelred's "virtuous" pre-monastic life as a steward in the court of King David of Scotland. Daniel's critics cited sections of Aelred's Mirror of Charity[51] and "Rule for a Recluse"[52] to buttress their displeasure. In these above-mentioned passages Aelred had mentioned some of his travails and regretted his involvement in secular pleasures in his early youth. In the Mirror of Charity, his first book, Aelred (having the Augustinian model safely before him) does confess his youthful lapses. However, in Aelred's self-disclosure there seems to be no desire to scandalize or titillate his readers nor is there a morbid desire for self-flagellation. He simply wishes to state that his own return from cupidity (misdirected love) to charity was a miracle of God's abiding grace.

In conclusion, the reflections of Geoffrey Webb and Adrian Walker seem to sum up the dominant themes and ambiance of Aelred's Mirror of Charity:

> ...the medieval speculum form is not that of a logically argued treatise. As Aelred says in this introductory letter to the abbot of Clairvaux, there are various themes running through it. It tends always to move spiralwise round its subject, carrying along in its course a host of ideas that might seem to be strictly speaking, irrelevant. The best way to read Aelred in the original is to allow oneself to drift along the movement of his contemplation, and one can at least suggest that the same method might best be followed when reading him in translation. A speculum (mirror) achieves its effect precisely by reflecting its subject matter from many different vantage points, and since it

is a more subjective piece of writing, the ultimate coordinating factor is, of course, the author's own personality. Aelred's genius for friendship is the thing that epitomizes his character, as his biographer and all the commentators on his work observe. God's right to man's love and the kinship that binds all creation together, are the fundamental intuitions that explain Aelred's concept of charity as concordia. As we listen to his words, and visualize him in the great Yorkshire monastery where he effected peace and love among his several hundred monks and brothers, we are struck by the all-embracing optimism of his ideas on friendship. He shares with his master, St. Bernard, a deep compassion for fallen mankind when his thoughts turn to the weighty matter of the soul's responsibility for sin. But he shares, too, the mentality of William of St. Thierry, who sought, in his Meditations for the light of God, and found it shining through the faces of the pure in heart.[53]

Notes to CHAPTER VI

1. See Powicke's introduction to Vita Ailredi, p. lviii.

2. See the Appendix to Aelred's Mirror of Charity (Speculum Caritatis), trans. Geoffrey Webb and Adrian Walker (London: A.R. Mowbray and Co., Ltd., 1962), p. 143.

3. Ibid., p. 15.

4. Ibid., p. 16, "Charity is spiritual circumcision."

5. Ibid., pp. 17-18. "Charity, the true Sabbath of the soul".

6. Ibid., p. 92.

7. Ibid., p. 118.

8. Ibid., p. 102.

9. Ibid., pp. 121-122.

10. Ibid., p. 136.

11. Ibid., p. 111.

12. *Ibid.*, pp. 72-76.

13. *Ibid.*, p. 3.

14. See Douglas Roby's introduction to Aelred's *Spiritual Friendship*, p. 14.

15. Aelred, *Mirror of Charity*, p. 145.

16. *Ibid.*

17. *Ibid.*

18. *Ibid.*, p. 60.

19. *Ibid.*

20. *Ibid.*, p. 61.

21. *Ibid.*, p. 62.

22. *Ibid.*

23. *Ibid.*

24. *Ibid.*

25. *Ibid.*, p. 63.

26. Matthew 24:45.

27. Aelred, *Mirror of Charity*, p. 63.

28. *Ibid.*, p. 64.

29. *Ibid.*, p. 68.

30. *Ibid.*, p. 69.

31. *Ibid.*, p. 70.

32. See the Appendix to *Mirror of Charity*, p. 143.

33. See Aelred's "Jesus at the Age of Twelve" in *Treatises and the Pastoral Prayer* (Kalamazoo, Michigan: Cistercian Publications, 1971), pp. 37-38.

34. Aelred, *Mirror of Charity*, p. 130.

35. See Appendix to *Mirror of Charity*, p. 153.

36. Aelred, *Mirror of Charity*, p. 8.

37. *Ibid.*, p. 3.

38. *Ibid.*

39. See Hallier's *The Monastic Theology of Aelred of Rievaulx* (Shannon, Ireland: Irish University Press, 1969), pp. 3-24.

40. Aelred, *Mirror of Charity*, p. 11.

41. *Ibid.*, p. 4.

42. *Ibid.*, pp. 14-15

43. *Ibid.*, p. 94.

44. *Ibid.*, p. 76.

45. *Ibid.*, pp. 101, 115-116, 137-141.

46. See Walter Daniel's *Vita Ailredi*, also see the appendix to this dissertation.

47. See the appendix to this dissertation. Also see Powicke's introduction to *Vita Ailredi*, pp. lix-lx, lxvi.

48. See St. Augustine's *Confessions*, Book 4.

49. St. Bernard had devoted most of his 26th sermon on the "Song of Songs" to lament the death of his brother, Gerard.

50. Aelred, *Mirror of Charity*, p. 138.

51. *Ibid.*, 1:79: "Et dicebant homines, attendentes quaedam circa me, sed nescientes quid ageretur in me: O quam bene est illi! O quam bene est illi! Ignorabant enim, quia ibi mihi male erat, ubi solum poterat bene esse. Valde enim intus erat plaga mea, crucians, terrens, et intolerabili fetore omnia interiora mea corrumpens; et nisi cito admouisses manum, non tolerans meipsum, forte pessimum desperationis remedium adhibuissem."

52. See Aelred's "Rule of Life for a Recluse" in
    Treatises and the Pastoral Prayer, pp. 93-96.

53. See G. Webb and A. Walker's introduction to Aelred's
    Mirror of Charity, p. xi.

CHAPTER VII

"JESUS AT THE AGE OF TWELVE"
("DE JESU PUERO DUODENNI")[1]

Aelred of Rievaulx's treatise "Jesus at the Age of Twelve" ("De Jesu Puero Duodenni") can pose initial difficulties, both of comprehension and of appreciation, to the modern reader. This treatise lacks intellectual incisiveness, methodical, linear progression of thoughts and, at times, seems highly colored by the author's subjectivity. However, a deeper, unhurried reading of this discursive meditation coupled with a "temporary suspension" of impatience (and the imposition of anachronistic standards) yields richer results, namely, clarity of comprehension and affection for "Jesus at the Age of Twelve."

David Knowles in his introduction to this treatise informs us:

> The treatise, "Jesus at the Age of Twelve" was written
> c. 1153-7 for his friend Ivo, a monk of Wardon, a daughter

house of Rievaulx in Bedfordshire. In addition to its
grace and charm it is an example of that devotion to
the human life of Christ that is a feature of religious
life in the twelfth and thirteenth centuries. Ailred
was not wholly original; he had before him the writings
of such men as John of Fécamp, St. Anselm and St. Bernard,
but in its careful schematization for the benefit of
Ivo's careful meditation, and its division into three
parts - the historical explanation, the moral lessons,
and the mystical interpretation - it stands in the
line of the meditations which prepared the way for
the affective prayer of later middle ages, which in
turn, by way of Rudolf of Saxony's Life of Christ and
Abbot Cisneros of Montserrat, led to the Exercises of
St. Ignatius.[2]

Aelred divides this treatise into three parts, following the acceptable literary canons of his time. Richard Winston reminds us that

> Literature had to be read with close attention to the
> three levels of meaning: historia, the literal sense;
> allegoria, the recondite, spiritual sense; and sententia,
> the implicit, moral sense.[3]

Aelred's "Jesus at the Age of Twelve" is more of a swirling étude full of "asides" than a systematic exegesis or a closely-knit, intellectual essay on a Biblical passage. Towards the end of the first section ("The Historical Sense") of this treatise, Aelred confesses to Ivo:

> ...what you are looking for, my son, is not theological
> speculation but devotion; not something to sharpen
> your tongue but something to arouse your affections.[4]

Moreover, the first section of this treatise ("The Historical Sense"), is not historically, i.e. factually and chronologically, informative. In this section Aelred's affective imagination seeks reasons for the boy Jesus's absence from his parents for three days and speculates on various plausible and metaphysical possibilities.

In spite of his innate graciousness and empathy for people of diverse temperaments and perspectives, Aelred was, nevertheless, a medieval man and an abbot - deeply convinced of the necessity of a "proper order" in life and interested in the maintenance of both secular and religious hierarchical patterns. Consequently Aelred encourages Ivo to perceive the boy Jesus as obedient and receptive to his elders, rather than a disconcerting lad

> ...he comes into the temple not as a teacher but as a boy who learns, who listens and asks questions, and in all this he does not withdraw himself from the control of his parents...

> ...In order to give a more clearly defined and outstanding example of humility and obedience and at the same time of readiness to give up one's own will and comply with the injunctions of elders...he disengaged himself from these sublime concerns, so useful and so necessary, to submit himself to the will of his parents in the words of the Evangelist: 'He went down with them and was subject to them.'[5]

Having emphasized the virtues of humility and deference to benign authorities, Aelred refers to one of his favorite parables, that of the Prodigal Son. He compares himself to the prodigal son and somewhat surprisingly likens those who have voluntarily embraced religious life to the animals who witnessed the birth of Jesus in the stable in Bethlehem.

Furthermore, Aelred assures Ivo that the human soul is sometimes bereft of spiritual consolations only to heighten the joy of its release into serenity, peace and gladness.

> Sitting in darkness and shadow of death, suffering from the absence of the sweetness we used to experience, bound and shackled with iron, that is, the hardness of our own hearts, we must needs cry out to the Lord in our tribulation and he will deliver us from our straights. For He scatters the darkness of this temptation with the light of His consolation and breaks the bonds of interior hardness by the grace of heartfelt compunction.[6]

Aelred allows himself to conjecture about the boy Jesus's activities during the three days that he was absent from his parents. He wonders whether Jesus was at that time giving families other than his own the comfort and solace of his presence or whether he was voluntarily experiencing the miseries of the mendicant by begging for his food? In an imaginative leap, attempting to reconcile the paradox of Jesus's humanity, as well as his divinity, Aelred wonders whether he was visiting the celestial realms during this absence of three days.

Aelred does not fail to discuss the informative and interpretative rôle played by Jesus, even as a boy. However, he adds a cautionary caveat for Ivo's benefit:

> This is an example of humility and modesty for boys and youths, teaching them to be silent in the midst of their elders, to listen and ask questions so as to learn.[7]

Aelred alludes to some of the seemingly endless theological arguments forwarded to defend and explain the paradox (or conundrum?) of Jesus's humanity and divinity. As a pious Cistercian abbot he subscribes to the notion that his Lord is perfect. However, as a humanist he affirms

> ...we confess that he was man not merely in appearance but truly. He possessed a truly human nature in which he could advance in years.[8]

It is characteristic of Aelred's innate catholicity, his willingness to give the opinions of his fellow human beings "root-room", his lack of stridency or harsh rigor towards those who differed from him and, above all, of his engaging humility, that in a single paragraph he shares his own convictions (based on his faith) but hastens to add,

> ...much has been said by many persons, each according to his own judgement and it is not for me to pronounce on their opinions...Everyone may judge of these opinions as he wills...it is for those to decide who are competent to discuss such matters.[9]

The first part of this treatise gives us many insights about his refusal to be embroiled in theological combats, his regard for "order", his respect for his superiors, his admiration for the virtues of humility, and deference to the needs of others, above all, the centrality of emphasis on <u>caritas</u> (in the sense of the soul's love and longing for God) in Aelred's life and thought.

The second part of Aelred's treatise on "Jesus at the Age of Twelve" is entitled "The Allegorical Sense." In this section Aelred continues his attempt to illustrate to Ivo the paradox of Jesus's humanity and divinity. Throughout this treatise Aelred tries to show the intrinsic link between the Creator and His creation, and emphasizes the rôle of God as exemplar, mentor and model.

Aelred does not offer his Lord polite homage from a distance. Instead, he regards Jesus not only as a paradigm of perfection but one who is fully human - consequently, a plausible guide who can be emulated, in Aelred's opinion.

Walter Daniel, Aelred's first biographer, had mentioned in Vita Ailredi that the abbot's favorite gospel was the one attributed to St. John.[10] Jesus's comments to Nicodemus seem to have been in the forefront of Aelred's mind when he wrote:

> Let his bodily birth then be the model of our spiritual birth, that is of conversion to holiness; the persecution that he suffered at the hands of Herod, a sign of the temptation that we undergo from Satan at the beginning of our conversion; his bringing up at Nazareth, the image of our advance in virtue.[11]

Moreover, the injunctions in the Sermon on the Mount and St. Bernard's comment[12] about the inversion of natural norms in religious life seem to echo through the following lines from Aelred's pen:

> He who is great became a little child, he who is rich became a poor baby; so that you who are great in your own eyes might become a little child through humility, you who are rich in your covetousness might become a poor baby...So are you born in Christ and so is Christ born in you.[13]

Aelred then proceeds to discuss the threefold path of purgation, illumination and union. Although this concept of the three stages of spiritual growth is far from original, Aelred's style is flavored with a fervor which suggests experiential knowledge of this threefold path and a sincere belief in its efficacy.

Aelred's innate optimism and faith in the reconciling power of God's love for humanity, led him to believe that the persecution of the Jews would soon come to an end. One may smile sorrowfully when encountering the naïve optimism of this twelfth century pleader of peace. Nevertheless, the words that Aelred (impelled by his deep desire for peace and justice) imputes to God, is a moving example of his own longing for reconciliation:

> I am calling back those whom I cast off, I am gathering together again those whom I scattered, I am welcoming those whom I rejected.[19]

In the third section of "Jesus at the Age of Twelve", entitled "The Moral Sense", Aelred seems to turn with relief (from the conundrums of the first and second parts of this treatise) to more familiar ground - i.e., a discourse on the affective and experiential aspects of a soul's spiritual journey in its quest for God.

Aelred quite explicitly tells Ivo the purpose of the final section of this treatise:

> Now I must come back to you, my dearest son...I hope to be able to explain your progress to you through this passage from the Gospel, so that you may read in these pages what you are experiencing in interior joy in yourself. For you have, I think, made the passage from the poverty of Bethlehem to the wealth of Nazareth, and, arriving at the age of twelve, you have gone up from the flowers of Nazareth to the fruits of Jerusalem. Thus you are able to study the hidden things of the spirit not so much in books as in your own experience.[20]

Aelred follows in "The Moral Sense" a traditional

Christian description of the three levels of spiritual unfoldment:

> For as Bethlehem, where Christ was born little and poor, is the beginning of a good life, and Nazareth, where he was brought up, is the practice of the virtues, so Jerusalem, to which he went up at the age of twelve, is the contemplation of heavenly secrets.[21]

There is nothing flat or formulaic about Aelred's description of the dynamics of the contemplative's quest for the Creator. Indeed, the fervor, urgency and realism of Aelred's descriptions of the inner journey attest to his personal experience of this process.

Aelred also elucidates for Ivo's benefit his (i.e. Aelred's) notions of God's power, wisdom and goodness. He assures Ivo that God, the "most powerful king" grants His regal protection to those who seek His aid. Aelred's spiritual optimism is reflected in his invincible faith that God does indeed grant to the questioning soul explanations for the anguish and iniquities which throng this world.

> But if you wish to have the knowledge of secrets or the solution of some problem revealed to you, if you wonder in bewilderment what explanation there can be for so much confusion in the world, if you are scandalized because you see sinners enjoying tranquility, exempt from the toil of men and not scourged with their afflictions, then you are seeking a retreat where you may be alone with Jesus and talk to him...When you ask such questions the Master will come to your side...He will come in the guise of a kind doctor. In his right hand he bears the flaming Law to enlighten you with knowledge of the Law and to set you afire with charity, which comes from meditation on the Law.[22]

Nevertheless, Aelred cautions Ivo against inquisitiveness:

> In his left hand there will be the rod of equity, and the sceptre with which he reigns, to charge you with presumption in your questioning and to bridle your curiousity.[23]

According to Aelred, an impassioned lover of God is not satisfied by the assurance of His regal omnipotence nor by an inkling of His omniscience. Aelred believed that the genuine pilgrim seeks the loving embrace of his/her Lord:

> Finally, if all these things, great as they are and splended and sublime, seem to be of no account since such is your longing for one kiss...and if you begin to complain in the Prophet's words: 'I have sought your face, your face, Lord, I seek'...then certainly He will come to you with all the fragrance of ointments and perfumes.[24]

Mary Magdelene[25] was regarded by medieval writers as an archetype of mortals' fallibility and of humans' potential for fervent faith, love and redemptive return to God. Aelred wrote with glowing sincerity of the transformation and spiritual ascent of the formerly erring, misguided soul:

> The first day, then, on which the soul that thirsts for God dwells in the delights of contemplation as if in Jerusalem, is the consideration of God's power. The second day is admiration of His wisdom. The third day is a sweet foretaste of His goodness and kindness. To the first belongs justice; to the second, knowledge; to the third mercy. Justice terrifies, knowledge teaches, mercy cherishes...And on the first day that fear which proceeds from the consideration of justice purifies the soul. When it has been purified wisdom enlightens it. When it has been enlightened goodness rewards it by communicating to it its sweetness...I know you will not be surprised that sorrow is not absent from what I have called delights, since you have often experienced that the sorrow which proceeds from chaste fear is preferred by the contrite soul to all the delights of this world.[26]

Two hundred years after Aelred wrote this treatise, another English monk, the anonymous author of The Cloud of Unknowing also spoke of the efficacy of sorrow[27] on the journey to Truth. This sorrow, however, is not akin to the griefs, discomforts or displeasures that one encounters in the treadmill of one's daily life. This is the soul's poignant awareness of its separation from God - an overwhelming, utter sorrow which is the prelude to grace, to the ineffable experience of "at-oneness" with one's Source. However, to mystics such as Aelred and Bernard such moments of grace are too brief:

> But alas, alas, it is a moment that comes but rarely and lasts only a very short time.[28]

The tone of this treatise suddenly changes. As if disconcerted by the extent of his self-disclosure, Aelred's natural modesty soon asserts itself. He hastens to add

> Our slight experience in the matter enables us to say as much as this. But men of more outstanding merit, endowed with greater talents and with souls better purified make more sublime and more profound discoveries in these three things. In God's power they see the depths of His judgements; in His wisdom, His hidden purposes; in His goodness, the unutterable words of His mercy.

However, this cautionary mood is soon replaced by further self-disclosure. Aelred's intense faith, coupled with his innate mysticism produce fervent prose.

> He who in spirit contemplates the things of the spirit is found not just anywhere in Jerusalem but in the temple. For Jerusalem has a courtyard, it has gates, it also has a temple. While the courtyard sometimes lies open even to enemies, the gates are opened only to friends and entrance into the temple is granted only to the perfect.

> The man who is able to see the eternal in the things of time, the heavenly in the earthly, the divine in the human, the Creator in the creature, may exult as if admitted to Jerusalem's courtyards.[30]

Aelred informs Ivo that intellectual prowess and exegetical acumen are not enough to warrant entry (metaphorically speaking) into the sanctuary of God's temple. Only one who is ignited by "interior love" for the Creator is worthy to enter the sanctuary of His temple.

> ...if upon the altar of your heart the flame of heavenly desire has set on fire the fatness of interior love and the marrow of your affections so that fragrant smoke mounts up from your burning prayers and your mind's eye extends its gaze into heaven's secret places while the palate of your heart tastes the blessed savor of God's own sweetness, then you have been in Jerusalem's temple and offered there a most acceptable offering.[31]

At the end of this treatise Aelred emphasizes the importance of maintaining a balance between the demands of a life of service to one's fellow mortals and the interior delights of prayer and contemplation:

> ...the eternal law commands us not wholly to neglect the contemplation of God for the sake of our neighbor's welfare, nor again to neglect our neighbor's welfare for the delights of contemplation.[32]

At this juncture, Aelred regards Joseph as the Holy Spirit, Mary as Charity and the boy Jesus as the representative of the soul which experiences the joys of contemplation, as well as a symbol of "those spiritual men, who have been entrusted with preaching God's Word and caring for souls."[33]

Aelred then gives us a vivid vignette of the demands and duties of an abbot of Rievaulx. His description is both specific and timeless. Without self-conciousness or priggishness he delineates the sacrifices that are necessary when a generous pastor is dedicated to a vocation of service:

> Therefore it is not without good reason that, if we indulge in repose more than is fitting, fraternal charity as it were complains of us. It is dissatisfied with our stay in Jerusalem if it feels that our repose is fraught with harm for others who depend upon our solicitude.
>
> For when we lay to one side all business to give ourselves to interior meditation or to private prayer, if we linger in such delights longer than is good for those under our care, the Spirit intervenes and charity prompts us. We suddenly remember the weak and take thought for this one in distress who is waiting for fatherly consolation, that one suffering temptation and wondering when his father will appear in public and bring him some comfort by his words. Another is provoked to anger and murmuring against his father because there is no one to whom he can make the confession that will heal him, ridding him of the poison he has imbibed. And there is yet another overcome by the spirit of spiritual weariness (acedia) running hither and thither to find someone to talk to and to advise him. It is by means of such promptings originating in our brethren's hearts, that we hear mother charity upbraiding us as it were: 'Son, why have you behaved so toward us? I and your father have been looking for you in sorrow.'
>
> ...But if the love of repose leads the soul's feelings to murmur against such necessities, as if to say: 'Ought I not to concern myself with my Father's business?'... Nonetheless the reasoning spirit considers...that he who lives may not live for himself.[34]

Aelred's innate graciousness and pastoral concern for his "sons", both collectively and individually, his belief in the efficacy of affectionate dialogue, his lack of hypocrisy and arrogance argue in favor of the "sanity and sanctity" that his close associates regarded as the characteristic qualities of the Abbot of Rievaulx.

Aelred had neither the dialectical skill of Abelard nor the theological acumen and thundering rhetoric of Bernard of Clairvaux. Aelred "was not a doctor of the Church, nor the hammer of popes and delinquent bishops. His was a pure and steady candle - flame; not a blaze that could light up a dark sky or consume a forest. Yet he had a personality unique among the writers and abbots of that age. Highly gifted, strong both to do and to suffer, he was an abbot whose wisdom appeared primarily in his personal love and wise direction of souls. As his disciple and biographer could say: He who loved us all was deeply loved by us in return, and counted this the greatest of his blessings."[35]

Notes to CHAPTER VII

1. Luke 2: 41-51.
   Also see H. DeLubac, *Exegese Medievale*, 4 vols., (Paris: Aubier, 1959-64).

2. See David Knowles' introduction to Aelred's *Treatises and Pastoral Prayer* (Kalamazoo, Michigan: Cistercian Publications, 1971), p. xi.

3. Richard Winston, *Thomas Becket* (New York: Alfred A. Knopf, Inc., 1967), p. 10.

4. Aelred, "Jesus at the Age of Twelve" in *Treatises and Pastoral Prayer*, pp. 13-14. Henceforth the abbreviation of this treatise will be "J.A.T."

5. *Ibid.*, pp. 6, 12.

6. *Ibid.*, p. 8.

7. *Ibid.*, p. 11.

8. *Ibid.*, p. 13.

9. *Ibid.*,

10. John 3: 1-14.

11. Aelred, "J.A.T.", p. 16.

12. See Bernard of Clairvaux, Letter 87, PL 182: col. 217 C-D; trans. James, letter 90, p. 135. Quoted by C. W. Bynum in *Jesus as Mother* (L.A.: Univ. of California Press, 1982), pp. 127-128:

> "A good sort of playing this...by which we become an object of reproach to the rich and of ridicule to the proud. In fact what else do seculars think we are doing by playing when what they desire most on earth we fly from; and what they fly from we desire? (We are) like acrobats and jugglers, who with heads down and feet up, stand or walk on their hands...And we too play this game that we may be ridiculed, discomfited, humbled, until he comes who puts down the mighty from their seats and exalts the humble."

13. Aelred, "J.A.T.", p. 16.

14. *Ibid.*, p. 21.

15. *Ibid.*, p. 20.

16. Jeremiah 2:8.

17. Isaiah 10:22.

18. Malachi 1:1.

19. Aelred, "J.A.T.", pp. 23-24.

20. *Ibid.*, p. 25.

21. *Ibid.*

22. *Ibid.*, pp. 31-32.

23. *Ibid.*, p. 32.

24. *Ibid.*

25. *Ibid.*, p. 33-35. Also see The Cloud of Unknowing, trans. Ira Progoff (New York: Dell Pub. Co., Inc., 1957), pp. 99-101.

26. Aelred, "J.A.T.", p. 35.

27. Cloud of Unknowing, pp. 161-163.

28. See Aelred, "J.A.T.", p. 30, n. 24: "'Rara hora et parva mora,' a play on words which evidently Aelred borrowed from Bernard of Clairvaux. See 'Sermon Twenty-three on the Song of Songs,' n. 15, The Works of Bernard of Clairvaux, vol. 2 (Cistercian Fathers Series 4)."

29. Aelred, "J.A.T.", pp. 35-36.

30. *Ibid.*, p. 36.

31. *Ibid.*

32. *Ibid.*, p. 37.

33. *Ibid.*

34. *Ibid.*, pp. 37-38.

35. See David Knowles' introduction to Aelred's Treatises and Pastoral Prayer, p. xi.

CHAPTER VIII

SPIRITUAL FRIENDSHIP
(DE SPIRITUALI AMICITIA)

The Prologue

Although it is easy to discover the palpable influence of St. Augustine's Confessions[1] in Aelred's prologue to his Spiritual Friendship (De Spirituali Amicitia), this preface does contain many authentically autobiographical elements which one has encountered earlier in The Mirror of Charity (Speculum Caritatis), "Jesus at the Age of Twelve" ("De Jesu Puero Duodenni") and "Rule for a Recluse" ("Institutione Inclusarum").

Aelred's was an intensely affective nature which evoked and responded to the reciprocity of friendship. Contemporary accounts (and inadvertent self-disclosures in his own work) indicate that Aelred was a gifted man of singular charm and refinement, one who was delighted by "cultivated conversations" and congenial company. Evidently, even as a boy, these traits were not lacking in his nature. Apparently, while still a lad, Aelred was often in a state of inner conflict in his search for an ethical application and appropriate "channeling" of his affections in authentic friendships:

> And so, torn between conflicting loves and friendships, I was drawn now here, now there, and not knowing the law of true friendship, I was often deceived by its mere semblance.[2]

Aelred discovered Cicero's De Amicitia as a youth, probably during his tenure as a favored courtier in the household of King David of Scotland. This book had a profound, life-long impact on Aelred who was unable to forget it even after he had discarded a promising career at court to become a Cistercian monk at Rievaulx, in Yorkshire. Without doubting the honesty of his intentions, it is unwise to accept literally at "face value" some of Aelred's statements (quoted below). Throughout his life, Aelred sought, not always successfully, to reconcile his humanistic interests (in this case his abiding affection for Cicero's De Amicitia and his love of scripture, saints' works and patristic material) with his vocation as a Cistercian monk. In a way, the following lines sound more like a vigorous Aelredian attempt to persuade himself that Christian scriptures were sufficient for his inner nurture, than a transcendence of his love of humanistic (particularly Ciceronian) literature:

> The ideas I had gathered from Cicero's treatise on friendship kept recurring to my mind, and I was astonished that they no longer had for me their wonted savor. For now nothing which had not been sweetened by the

honey of the most sweet name of Jesus, nothing which had not been seasoned with the salt of Sacred Scripture, drew my affection so entirely to itself. Pondering over these thoughts again and again, I began to ask myself whether they could perhaps have some support from Scripture.[3]

It has been observed by some scholars that Cistercians gave up everything except the art of writing well.[4] After reading and reflecting on spiritual literature germane to the theme of friendship, Aelred decided to write his "own book on spiritual friendship" and to define for himself "rules for a chaste and holy love." Since he was an abbot writing for an immediate monastic[5] audience, Aelred felt that it was imperative for him to indicate that his work was quite distinct from the genre of romance, of tales of knightly[6] combat and camaraderie. This genre of courtly literature was infiltrating the craggy, ascetical reaches of northern England from southern France - the sunny domain of one of England's most memorable queens, Eleanor of Acquitaine.

In spite of his affective nature and courtly refinement, Aelred of Rievaulx was a practical man, realistic enough to realize that increasing ill health and the steady, often unpredictable, demands of his abbatial duties would prevent him from giving this work the benefit of his undivided attention. The craftsman in him was dissatisfied by his inability to give this book the solicitude of detailed attention. Consequently, he ruefully warns his readers "if anyone deems that I have written superfluous or impractical, let him pardon my unhappy position whose occupations forced me to put limits to the thought I could give to this meditation."[7]

Book 1

Spiritual Friendship (De Spirituali Amicitia) is cast in the form of a dialogue between Aelred and some of his spiritual "sons". The first part of Spiritual Friendship is the record of a conversation between the author and Ivo of Wardon, at whose request Aelred had written his treatise "Jesus at the Age of Twelve". The opening lines express Aelred's gratitude and delighted appreciation of a quiet conversation with a friend - a rare interlude of privacy amidst the swirl of his constant duties as abbot, arbitrator, administrator, pastor, preacher, author and ecclesiastical ambassador. Aelred tells Ivo:

> Here we are, you and I, and I hope a third, Christ, is in our midst. There is no one now to disturb us; there is no one to break in upon our friendly chat, no man's prattle or noise of any kind will creep into this pleasant solitude. Come now, beloved, open your heart, and pour into these friendly ears whatsoever you will, and let us accept gratefully the boon of this place, time, and leisure.[8]

However, the conversation is not merely a carefree interchange among peers but a deeply reflective dialogue between a questing monk and his perceptive pastor. As indicated by Ivo's words, Aelred was aware of his (Ivo's) disquiet and his need to communicate quietly with his abbot.

Ivo, as presented in this dialogue, may be less of a portrait of the actual monk of Wardon (although one cannot overrule this possibility) than a literary creation, a convenient mouthpiece who expresses Aelred's own queries, dilemmas and hopes in his persistent search for a synthesis between his humanistic interests and his vocation as a Cistercian monk. As Aelred's alter ego, Ivo wants Cicero's reflections on friendship to be corroborated by the scriptures. Moreover, the christocentric Ivo hesitates to impute to Cicero the knowledge of authentic friendship "since he (Cicero) was completely unaware of its beginning and end, Christ." Since Ivo wished to approach the theme of spiritual friendship in "an ordered discussion" he requests of Aelred insights into "the nature of friendship." True to his own persistent love of Cicero's classic, Aelred suggests a sentence from De Amicitia[9] ("Friendship is mutual harmony in affairs human and divine coupled with benevolence and charity") as a starting point.

Ivo, however, is not entirely satisfied by Aelred's explanation of the above-mentioned quotation from De Amicitia. He seeks to understand its implications in a more specific manner:

> I grant that this definition pleases me adequately, except that I should think it applied equally to pagans and Jews, and even to bad Christians. However, I am convinced that true friendship cannot exist among those who live without Christ.[10]

It is a measure of Aelred's genuine catholicity and literary finesse that he parries Ivo's comment both gracefully and prudently. He does not allow himself to be trapped into either religious chauvinism or self-congratulatory rhetoric,

Nor does he open himself to charges of heresy (and its concomitants - trial by ordeal and death by torture) by a blunt avowal of his unfettered <u>agape</u>. Instead of embroiling himself in the dangerous cauldron of divisive religious dogma, Aelred preferred to elucidate the key terms in the vocabulary of friendship. He tells Ivo:

> I shall be glad to comply with your wishes if only you will pardon my lack of knowledge and not force me to teach what I do not know. Now, I think the word <u>amicus</u> (friend) comes from the word <u>amor</u> (love), and <u>amicitia</u> (friendship) from <u>amicus</u>. For love is a certain "affection" of the rational soul whereby it seeks and eagerly strives after some object to possess it and enjoy it. Having attained its object through love, it enjoys it with a certain interior sweetness, embraces it, and preserves it. We have explained the affections and movements of love as clearly and carefully as we could in our <u>Mirror</u> with which you are already familiar.[11]

Quoting from the Book of Proverbs and the Psalms of the Hebrew Bible, from the New Testament, and from the Church Fathers, Aelred tries to show Ivo that genuine friendship is an expression of altruism and shared, self-sacrificial, religious faith - qualities which he admits are rarely found among the pagans.

Ivo's query ("Are we then to believe that there is no difference between charity and friendship?") enables Aelred to elucidate a matter on which he had evidently spent much thought. In his first book, the <u>Mirror of Charity</u>, this difference is described in a number of ways - both metaphors and narrative expositions are used by Aelred to delineate the qualities and responsibilities that pertain to charity and friendship.' In <u>De Spirituali Amicitia</u>, Aelred expresses his views on this subject more concisely and simply, distilling in a paragraph the reflections of a lifetime. Aelred answers Ivo's above-mentioned question with frankness:

> On the contrary, there is a vast difference; for divine authority approves that more are to be received into the bosom of charity than into the embrace of friendship. For we are compelled by the law of charity to receive in the embrace of love not only our friends but also our enemies. But only those do we call friends to whom we can fearlessly entrust our heart and all its secrets; those, too, who, in turn, are bound to us by the same law of faith and security.[12]

The medieval love of the triad expresses itself in Aelred's response to Ivo's request for a catalogue of types of friendship, so that the nature of "spiritual friendship" can be clearer by contrast. Aelred allows a hesitant, conditional appellation of "friendship" to unspiritual affiliations, for the sake of discussion and analysis:

> Let us allow that, because of some similarity in feelings, those friendships which are not true, be, nevertheless, called friendships, provided, however, they are judiciously distinguished from that friendship which is spiritual and therefore true. Hence let one kind of friendship be called carnal, another worldly, and another spiritual. The carnal springs from mutual harmony in vice; the worldly is enkindled by the hope of gain; and the spiritual is cemented by similarity of life, morals, and pursuits among the just.[13]

In spite of Aelred's liberal use of Biblical and patristic references, his descriptions and evaluations of "carnal" and "worldly" affiliations (i.e. false friendships) closely follow

Cicero's analysis in De Amicitia. The thirst for sensual pleasure and temporal gain was abhorrent to Aelred. Aelred's remarks reveal not only intellectual accord with the thoughts of the great Roman orator but visceral assent.

Moreover, Aelred's descriptions and definitions of the calibre of the participants in spiritual friendship, their motive and reward, also reflect his close adherence to Cicero's De Amicitia.[14]

In response to Ivo's question regarding the genesis of friendship, Aelred again draws upon De Amicitia.[15] However, true to his vocation as a Cistercian abbot, Aelred also cites scriptural[16] references, as well as ancient and (his) contemporary, Christian, magisterial sources, such as St. Augustine and Bernard of Clairvaux.[17]

Part I of Aelred's De Spirituali Amicitia is noted (like Parts II and III) for its synthesis of classical and Christian elements, its polished prose and its cadenced conclusion. However, Aelred does not allow his readers to be lulled by the beauty of his style. This medieval abbot injected into his work a daring piece of his personal conviction - namely, the equality of the sexes.

> Finally, when God created man, in order to commend more highly the good of society, He said: "It is not good for man to be alone: let us make him a helper like unto himself." It was from no similar, nor even from the same, material that divine Might formed this help mate, but as a clearer inspiration to charity and friendship He produced the woman from the very substance as the man. How beautiful it is that the

second human being was taken from the side of the first, so that nature might teach that human beings are equal and, as it were, collateral, and that there is in human affairs neither a superior nor an inferior, a characteristic of true friendship.[18]

In the concluding section of the first part of <u>De Spirituali Amicitia</u>, Aelred is able to overcome Ivo's reluctance to accord friendship the respect due to wisdom. Using persuasive scriptural, as well as patristic definitions of friendship, Aelred asserts that charity and friendship are interlinked,

> Since...in friendship eternity blossoms, truth shines forth, and charity grows sweet, consider whether you ought to separate the name of wisdom from these three.[19]

On hearing his eulogy Ivo tries to venture an audacious equation: "God is friendship." However, Aelred is too careful a churchman to encourage such a comment. He cautions Ivo:

> That would be unusual, to be sure, nor does it have the sanction of the Scriptures. But still what is true of charity, I surely do not hesitate to grant to friendship, since "he that abides in friendship, abides in God, and God in him."[20]

It is a measure of the balance of "sanctity and sanity"[21] in Aelred's nature that he was able to compose in a variety of keys. From the rarefied atmosphere of a discussion about the nature and nuances of spiritual friendship, the first book closes on an intensely human note which has a touch of wry humor. Ivo complains with frank peevishness (as Aelred graciously but firmly concludes the dialogue and returns to the daily demands of his abbatial duties):

> I admit that my eagerness finds such a delay quite annoying, but it is necessary since not only is it time for the evening meal, from which no one may be absent, but, in addition, there are the burdensome demands of the other religious who have a right to your care.[22]

SPIRITUAL FRIENDSHIP

(DE SPIRITUALI AMICITIA)

Book II

The mood and tone characteristic of Aelred's "discursive meditation" continues in the second part of De Spirituali Amicitia. The theme of this section is "the fruition and excellence of friendship."[23] In spite of this homilitic title, this second section begins on a note of *badinage* between Aelred and his future biographer, Walter Daniel.

Although cognizant of Walter's impatient contempt for the abbot's administrative duties and necessary "interchanges" with secular officials, Aelred queries him with gentle humor:

> Come here now, brother, and tell me why you were sitting all alone a little while ago at some distance from us, when I was dealing with material affairs with those men of the flesh. There you were, turning your eyes now this way, now that; then you would rub your forehead with your hand; presently you would run your fingers through your hair; again, frowning angrily, you would, with all sorts of faces, complain that something quite apart from your own desires had happened to you.[24]

Walter, according to Aelred's depiction, remained impervious to his abbot's humor, preferring to retain his own querulous and somewhat sanctimonious standpoint:

> You have described the situation perfectly. For who could preserve his patience through a whole day seeing those agents of Pharaoh getting your full attention, while we, to whom you are particularly indebted, were not able to gain even so much as a word with you?[25]

True to his vocation as a teacher, Aelred was forced to give Walter explicit, practical advice:

> But we must show kindness to such people, too, for either we expect benefits from them or we fear their enmity.[26]

Moreover, one notices the blend of self-disclosure, empathetic advice, classical scholarship, pastoral care and conviviality that characterizes Aelred's writings:

> But since the doors have finally closed upon them, solitude is more gratifying to me now, in proportion as that preceding disturbance was distressing. You know, "the best appetizer is hunger"[27] and neither honey nor any other spice gives such relish to wine as strong thirst does to water. And so perhaps this conference of ours, like spiritual food and drink, will be more enjoyable to you because of the intense longing preceding it. Come now, and do not delay proposing to me what you were preparing to unravel from your troubled heart a little while ago.[28]

The interchange between Aelred and Walter which follows the above-mentioned quotation, throws a great deal of light on their respective characters and perspectives. Walter speaks to Aelred in an insistent, interrogative manner, eager to glean from him his thoughts on spiritual friendship.

Aelred, on the other hand, initially responds to Walter's intellectual urgency in an affective, reflective, anecdotal manner. Through the alchemy of memory, the presence of Aelred's late friend, Ivo, is still tangible in Aelred's life. Perhaps a reluctance to expose the manuscript of his precious conversation on spiritual friendship with Ivo, led Aelred to ward off Walter's importunities:

> But you know that very many years have passed since we lost that bit of paper on which I had written his questions and my answers on spiritual friendship.[29]

However, Walter's eager insistence, bolstered by his access to confidential information, cannot be dissuaded by Aelred's gentle reluctance to avoid exposure. He importunes Aelred with tenacity:

> The facts do not escape me, but to be candid, all my eagerness and impatience arise from the fact that I have heard from certain individuals that this very paper was found and handed over to you three days ago. Please, show it to your son, for my spirit will not rest until I have reviewed the whole discussion and see what is still wanting in it, and then present to your fatherly examination for rejection or acceptance or explanation whatever my own mind or secret inspiration suggest to me as matters requiring discussion.[30]

True to his generous, gracious nature Aelred agrees to share the contents of his manuscript with Walter but adds a cautionary caveat:

> I shall comply with your wishes, but I desire that you alone should read what is written on it, and that it not be brought to public attention. For I may, perhaps, decide that some points are to be omitted, some added, and, surely, many to be corrected.[31]

After a pause in the text which indicates a brief passage of time, Walter and his abbot are again presented in conversation with one another. In his characteristically impetuous, pugnaciously pragmatic manner, Walter (who has just read the first book of Aelred's Spiritual Friendship) wants to know

> what practical advantages it procures for those who cultivate it. For though it is a matter of moment... yet it is only when its purpose and benefit are understood that it will be sought after with genuine ardor.[32]

Aelred's response to Walter's query is a passage of symphonic beauty. Using both scriptural and classical allusions, Aelred attempts to convey to his intensely pragmatic student something of the beauty and the necessity of spiritual friendship. Aelred goes so far as to say

> scarcely any happiness whatever can exist among mankind without friendship, and a man is to be compared to a beast if he has no one to rejoice with him in adversity, no one to whom to unburden his mind if any annoyance crosses his path or with whom to share some unusually sublime or illuminating inspiration..."Woe to him that is alone, for when he falls, he has none to lift him up."[33] He is entirely alone who is without a friend.[34]

It is interesting to note that there is a contrapuntal quality to Aelred's dialogues. Instead of an exegesis of a Johannine passage which Aelred had just cited to Walter (Jn. 15:15), the tone shifts to encounter and inclusion of persons in the present tense. Gratian, one of the residents of Rievaulx, "drops in" unannounced to enjoy a conversation with Aelred. However, there is a decided "edge" in the conversation between Walter and Gratian. In a way, this interchange has the qualities of a comedy of situation. Walter had just professed to his abbot an extravagant adulation of friendship:

> I confess your words have so moved me and so enkindled my soul to a burning desire for friendship, that I believe I am not even alive as long as I am deprived of the manifold benefits of this great good. But what you said last, the statement which aroused me so completely and almost carried me away from all earthly things, I desire to hear developed more fully, namely, that among the stages leading to perfection friendship is the highest.[35]

However, as soon as an opportunity for amity concretely presents itself, with the entry of Gratian, Walter resorts to avuncular, condescending advice:

> It is opportune that he (Gratian) came along, since he might be too eager for friendship and be deceived by its mere semblance, mistake the counterfeit for the true, the imaginary for the real, the carnal for the spiritual.[36]

Gratian parries Walter's comments with irony. However, he clearly indicates his interest in Aelred's perspectives on spiritual friendship.

In attempting to elucidate how "friendship is, so to speak, a stage toward the love and knowledge of God," Aelred again refers to the Bible[37] and to Cicero's *De Amicitia*[38] with unselfconscious ease. He describes spiritual friendship in Ciceronian terms:

> Indeed, in friendship there is nothing dishonorable, nothing deceptive, nothing feigned; whatever there is, is holy, voluntary and true.[39]

However, in the succeeding sentence he refers to 2 Cor.:13 to emphasize that genuine, hence unselfish love, is indeed an important ingredient of friendship. His attempt to present a "synthesis" of his Christian - classical concept of friendship also includes a humane realism, a practical-pastoral note that is characteristic of Aelred of Rievaulx:

> Therefore, in the perfection of charity we love very many who are a source of burden and grief to us, for whose interest we concern ourselves honorably, not with hypocrisy or dissimulation, but sincerely and voluntarily, but we do not admit these to the intimacy of our friendship.[40]

For Aelred, unlike many of his co-religionists, friendship with fellow-mortals was not a hindrance to spiritual life. According to Aelred, friendship both facilitates and accelerates one's love of God. In spite of his unusually liberal views, it is not surprising, indeed, it is in character, that this Cistercian abbot should speak of Christ with intense love and reverence when elucidating his concept of spiritual friendship to monks who lived in the ambiance of his guidance.

> And so, in friendship are joined honor and charm, truth and joy, sweetness and good-will, affection and action. And all these take their beginning from Christ, advance through Christ and are perfected in Christ. Therefore, not too steep or unnatural does the ascent appear from Christ, as the inspiration of the love by which we love our friend, to Christ giving himself to us as our Friend for us to love, so that charm may follow upon charm, sweetness upon sweetness and affection upon affection. And thus, friend cleaving to friend in the spirit of Christ, is made with Christ but one heart and one soul...[41]

Like his contemporaries - Bernard of Clairvaux and William of St. Thierry, Aelred, too, was greatly attracted to the "Song of Songs" as a paradigm of the description of the soul's yearning for God.

Aelred generally avoided allegorical digressions in Spiritual Friendship, preferring to remain within a dialogical structure in this book. However, Aelred did interject something of an allegorical interlude and exegesis when commenting on the first line of the Song of Songs: "Let him kiss me with the kiss of his mouth." Aelred observes:

> There is, then, a corporeal kiss, a spiritual kiss, and an intellectual kiss. The corporeal kiss is made by the impression of the lips; the spiritual kiss by the union of spirits; the intellectual kiss through the Spirit of God, by the infusion of grace.[42]

Aelred then mentions the "worthy reasons" for which the "corporal kiss" can be exchanged - between relatives, friends, guests, spouses, co-worshippers - as a sign of affection, affirmation, welcome and peace. However, in a characteristically Cistercian manner Aelred expresses his disapproval and disgust of the "misuse" of the "corporeal kiss" when it is appropriated as an "agent of lust". The "spiritual kiss", according to Aelred, is

> characteristically the kiss of friends who are bound by one law of friendship; for it is not made by contact of the mouth but by affection of the heart; not by a meeting of lips but by a mingling of spirits, by a purification of all things in the Spirit of God.[43]

Aelred believed, however, that the "spiritual kiss", though generated by grace, is not yet the highest bliss.

For Aelred, the "intellectual kiss"[44] occurs when "all thoughts and desires which savor of the world have been quieted."[45]

Aelred again uses the device of conversation to add variety, tone and color to this work. Instead of continuing his exegesis and either boring the reader with repetition or falling into the trap of bathos - a fresh note of candor and questing, (as well as rivalry), is brought forth through Aelred's record of an interchange between Gratian and Walter. The former expresses surprise and bewilderment on hearing Aelred's description of spiritual friendship. Gratian frankly states that hitherto he

> believed friendship was nothing else than so complete an identity of wills between two persons that the one would wish nothing which the other did not wish.[46]

Walter, on the other hand, voices a plethora of opinions regarding the limits of friendship - many of which are discussed by Cicero in De Amicitia. True to his pragmatic, keenly practical nature, Walter states that

> we are trying to set up for ourselves a definite limit on how far friendship ought to go, since in this matter there is a difference of opinion among various individuals.[47]

Aelred does not immediately disclose to them the gamut of his reflections on the boundaries of friendship. He initially reiterates a passage from the New Testament:

> Greater love than this no man hath, that a man lay down his life for his friends.[48]

However, Walter is not satisfied by this response.

He interrogates Aelred closely:

> But if the wicked or pagans take such joy in the mutual harmony of evil and wickedness that they are willing to die for one another, shall we grant that they have reached the zenith of friendship?[49]

Naturally, Walter's question receives a firm answer in the negative: "Heaven forbid, since friendship cannot exist among the wicked." Aelred eventually consents to give a fuller explanation when Gratian (who possessed a gracious temperament akin to that of his abbot) requests a response. Then, Aelred succinctly summarizes his position:

> I shall tell you in a few words. It (i.e. spiritual friendship) can begin among the good, progress among the better and be consummated among the perfect. For as long as anyone delights in an evil thing from a desire of evil, as long as sensuality is more gratifying than purity, indiscretion than moderation, flattery than correction, how can it be right for such a one even to aspire to friendship, when it springs from an esteem for virtue? It is difficult, nay, impossible, for you to taste its beginnings, if you do not know the fountain from which it can spring. For that love is shameful and unworthy of the name of friendship wherein anything foul is demanded of a friend... Therefore, one ought to detest the opinion of those who think that one should act on behalf of a friend in a way detrimental to faith and uprightness. For it is no excuse for sin, that you sin for the sake of a friend.[50]

True to his commitment to attempt a classical - Christian synthesis, Aelred refers to Cicero's De Amicitia,[51] to the Bible[52] and to ecclesiastical events[53] of his time to elucidate his conviction that friendship is possible only "among the good."

Aelred allays Gratian's anxiety ("What then has friendship to do with us who are not good?") by characteristically using both classical and Christian definitions:

> We call a man "good" who, according to the limits of our mortality, "living soberly and justly and godly in this world," is resolved neither to ask others to do wrong nor to do wrong himself at another's request. Among such, indeed, we do not doubt that friendship can spring up and that by such it can be perfected.[54]

Walter, then, succinctly summarizes the Stoics' position, wondering whether friendship was worth the expenditure of one's anguish and anxiety, caused by concern for another's weal and woe.

Gratian becomes Aelred's mouthpiece in condemning the sophist's self-centered, opportunistic stance towards his fellow-mortals:

> We have been laboring in vain, then,...if we can so easily withhold ourselves from the desire of friendship, the fruit of which is so holy, so useful, so acceptable to God, and so near to perfection and recommended to us in so many ways. Let us leave the opinion you have spoken of to the man who wishes today's love to be such that it may turn into hatred tomorrow; who wishes to be the friend of all without trusting any; who praises today and reviles tomorrow; who flatters today and criticizes tomorrow; who today is prepared for kisses and tomorrow is ready for reproaches. The love of such a man is acquired at a small price, and at the slightest offence it disappears.

Aelred again employs his characteristic blend of Biblical and Ciceronian references, as well as his own practical, pastoral observations to refute the viewpoints of both the Stoics and the sophists regarding the value of friendship. An uncharacteristic, sharp note enters Aelred's response to Walter's importunities:

> Take your own life - does prudence struggle against error,

temperance against wantonness, justice against cunning, fortitude against cowardice, without any great anxiety on your part? Who, I ask, among men, especially among the young, is able to preserve his purity or restrain his sensual appetite without very great grief or fear?[56]

This vein of reprimand continues, no doubt to the surprise and discomfort of Walter, Aelred's future biographer:

> Paul must have been a fool, for he was unwilling to live without care and solicitude for others; but for the sake of charity which he believed to be the sovereign virtue, he was weak with the weak, on fire with the scandalized. And too, great sorrow was his and continual grief of heart on behalf of his brethren in the flesh... You see how those seek to take virtues out of the world who fear not to take solicitude, their associate, from our midst. Was it to no purpose that Chusai, the Arachite, preserved with such great fidelity his friendship with David, that he preferred anxiety, and would rather share the griefs of his friend than to relax amid the joys and honors of the parricide? I would say those men are beasts rather than human beings who declare that a man ought to live in such a way as to be to no one a source of consolation, to no one a source even of grief or burden; to take no delight in the good fortune of another, to impart to others no bitterness because of their own misfortune, caring to cherish no one and to be cherished by no one.[57]

Aelred concludes his admonition by denouncing (à la Cicero) those

> who think of friendship as a trade; for such with their lips only declare themselves friends when the hope of some temporal advantage favors them or when they try to make their friend an accomplice in some sort of base deed.[58]

Surprised and momentarily chastened by this uncharacteristic rebuke, Walter quietly seeks to know "what sort of friendship we ought to avoid and what sort we ought to cherish and preserve."[59]

Aelred, consequently, warns both Walter and Gratian of the dangers of immature, irrational affiliations which can easily cloud one's commonsense and deflect one into "concupiscence." Spiritual friendship, according to Aelred, is very different from this unthinking, coltish familiarity. He states that

> the beginnings of spiritual friendship ought to possess, first of all, purity of intention, the direction of reason and the restraint of moderation; and thus the very desire for such friendship, so sweet as it comes upon us, will presently make friendship itself a delight to experience, so that it will never cease to be properly ordered.[60]

Aelred gives no credence whatever to "friendship which is based on a likeness in evil." Since he had reiterated throughout De Spirituali Amicitia that friendship is only possible among the "good", Aelred's refusal to regard the complicity among criminals as "friendship", is hardly surprising.

Aelred then explores the concept of utilitarian friendship and comes to the conclusion that "he has not yet learnt what friendship is who wishes any reward other than itself."[61] As observed earlier, his exposition on "spiritual friendship" is threaded with references to the Bible (particularly the friendship between David and Jonathan)[62] and to Cicero's De Amicitia. However, a gracious geniality of tone which is so characteristic of Aelred, prevents the reader from regarding his work as a strange collage of disparate and dissonant elements:

> Since, therefore, among the good, friendship always precedes and advantage follows, surely, it is not so much the benefit obtained through a friend that delights as the friend's love in itself.[63]

At the end of Book II, Aelred sums up the principal aspects of this second section of his Spiritual Friendship. Gration, however, seeks further clarification:

> And now, please tell us what limit should be preserved in serving one's friends, and what caution should be kept in mind?[64]

With an engaging practicality which enabled him to be both an affective and an effective abbot, Aelred returns his eager students (Walter and Gration) to the needs and realities of the present moment:

> Both these and other matters pertaining to friendship remain to be discussed. But an hour has already passed, and these others who have just arrived are by their impatience, as you see, hustling me off to other business.[65]

Book II of Aelred's Spiritual Friendship ends with Walter's words. Walter's tone towards Aelred is both tenacious and respectful, complaining and hopeful:

> You may be sure I leave unwillingly. Tomorrow, indeed, when occasion presents itself, I intend to return. And let our friend Gratian see to it that he is on time tomorrow morning, so that he may not accuse us of neglect, or we accuse him of tardiness.[66]

The abbot of Rievaulx was not only a "good physician" to those under his spiritual care but a fine literary craftsman as well. He concludes this middle section with clarity, yet leaves the reader with enough suspense, so that s/he approaches the final section with pleasurable anticipation.

SPIRITUAL FRIENDSHIP
DE SPIRITUALI AMICITIA

Book III

In the final section of Spiritual Friendship (De Spirituali Amicitia), Aelred discusses with Gratian and Walter "conditions and characters requisite for unbroken friendship."[67] The opening line of the third part of Spiritual Friendship (Aelred: "Where have you come from and why have you come?") reminds one more of a koan (riddle) from a Zen abbot, than the gentle graciousness, one generally associates with Aelred of Rievaulx. In spite of Aelred's rather general comment at the conclusion of the second part of Spiritual Friendship ("other matters pertaining to friendship remain to be discussed"), Walter had aggressively appointed the following day for continuing the discussion. Aelred's above-mentioned question expresses a firmness of tone which indicates pique, discourages over-familiarity and is disconcerting for two reasons - it expresses a tenor which is uncharacteristic of him, and secondly, the answers to his two-fold question must have been apparent to him.

Gratian responds with comprehensible surprise: "Surely you know why I am here." Again, Aelred keeps his eager young disciple at arm's length with yet another query: "Do you want to follow up the questions which have been proposed?" He also attempts to dispel some of the angularity which Walter feels towards Gratian. He tells Walter: "Gratian is more friendly to you than you thought."

Unmollified by either Aelred's humor or affection, Walter, with his usual pragmatic insistence, seeks to have his mental curiosity satisfied on the subject of spiritual friendship.

Aelred's description of the intrinsic foundation of friendship is worth quoting:

> The fountain and source of friendship is love. There can be love without friendship but friendship without love is impossible.[68]

Moreover, Aelred describes different aspects of love:

> Love proceeds either from nature, or from duty, from reason alone, or from affection alone, and sometimes from both simultaneously...[69]

He clearly favors, however, the amalgam of affection and reason - e.g. when one is drawn to another by the moral excellence of character and balance of temperament rather than by the attraction of physical beauty or mental titillation.

In spite (or because) of his classical education, his aristocratic background and his sound knowledge of scripture, of allegorical and exegetical methods, as well as patristics, Aelred never lost his ability to express himself simply and to the point on matters of crucial importance. Aelred responds with clarity and directness to Walter's question whether everyone should be admitted to the "sweet mystery of friendship":

> In the first place, one ought to lay a solid foundation for spiritual love itself, and in this foundation its principles ought to be set down, so that those who are mounting straight up to its higher levels may not neglect or go beyond its foundation, but observe the greatest caution. That foundation is the love of God.[70]

According to Aelred, everything else, all affiliations and friendships, no matter how attractive, uplifting or innocuous, must be referred to this touchstone - the love of God - "to be brought back into conformity with its plan and set right according to its nature."[71]

Aelred's practical sagacity manifests itself in his reiteration, both in *The Mirror of Charity* and in *Spiritual Friendship* that "not all whom we love should be received into friendship, for not all are found worthy of it."[72] Following the classical concept that "friends have all things in common", Aelred counsels care, prudence, deliberation, before engaging oneself in the life-long affiliation of friendship. Aelred summarizes his advice to Gratian and Walter by recommending:

> the four stages by which one climbs to the perfection
> of friendship: the first is selection, the second
> probation, the third admission, the fourth perfect
> harmony in matters human and divine with charity and
> benevolence.[73]

Moreover, in response to Walter's query whether this definition (quoted above) is germane to "many types of friendship," Aelred emphatically asserts that these four stages are only applicable to "that friendship which is true," i.e. spiritual friendship among "the good who can exhibit neither wish nor action detrimental to faith or good morals."[74] Aelred then explicitly counsels his students to avoid friendship with "the irascible, the fickle, the suspicious, and the garrulous."[75] However, this advice exposes him to further scrutiny from both Walter and Gratian. Walter reminds his abbot of his "deep devotion" to his late, irascible friend. Aelred defends his former friendship by mentioning that the faults of his friend were not serious enough to "dissolve and break friendship," moreover, "if it happens that we have received such men into our friendship, we must bear with them patiently."[76]

Gration's observations are even more explicit than that of Walter. He refers to Aelred's friendship with another irascible person, at whom, he said, many look askance.

Again, Aelred employs the same argument - assuring them that

> Having once received him into my friendship, I can
> never do otherwise than love him...And since there

> was no question of any dishonor being involved, and
> as confidence was not violated, or virtue lessened,
> it was right for me to yield to my friend that I
> might bear with him when he seemed to have trans-
> gressed, and that, when his peace was endangered,
> I might prefer his will to mine.[77]

Although Walter expresses his reservations about Aelred's somewhat surprising choice of friends, he yet asks his abbot to specify "those five vices by which friendship is so injured as to be dissolved..."[78]

Aelred's deep love and intimate knowledge of the Bible is reflected in his response to Walter's request. Quoting from the book of Sirach, in the Apocrypha, Aelred answers:

> "For", says Scripture, "there may be a reconciliation
> with your friend except in the case of upbraiding,
> reproach, pride, disclosing of secrets or a treacherous
> wound; for in all these cases a friend will flee away."[79]

Using scriptural references and practical, pastoral advice, Aelred then illustrates the problems which arise from friendship with each of these five kinds of people (mentioned above). Aelred's concluding remark, reinforced by a quotation from Ambrose, summarizes his exhortations on the avoidance of incompatible affiliations:

> It is particularly advantageous for you to choose one
> who conforms to your habits, who harmonizes with your
> disposition. "Indeed, among dissimilar characters,"
> as blessed Ambrose remarks, "friendship cannot exist;
> therefore, the grace of each ought to be mutually con-
> sonant."[80]

Walter is puzzled by these stipulations and asks in amazement where such a paragon of a friend can be discovered:

> But where can such a man be found, one who is neither
> irascible, nor unstable, nor suspicious? For as to
> the over-talkative man, he cannot escape notice.[81]

Aelred's definition of a worthy friend, like his description of a "good" person, does not strain one's credulity, for his understanding is informed by commonsense, as well as idealism:

> Although it is not easy to find one who is never moved
> by these passions, there surely are many who are found
> to be superior to all of them; men who suppress anger
> with patience, restrain levity by preserving gravity,
> drive out suspicions by the contemplation of love.
> I should say that such men ought to be chosen by
> preference for friendship on the ground that they are
> better trained in it. Because they conquer vice with
> virtue, their friendship is the more enduring as their
> resistance to temptation is the more valiant.[82]

Aelred has unflinchingly recorded for posterity the persistent, frank interrogation which he permitted his monks to direct towards himself. Aelred has woven into his <u>Spiritual Friendship</u> an interesting interplay of exchange between Gratian, Walter and himself. Gratian, for example, returns to his earlier comment regarding Aelreds' irascible friends - thus forcing his mentor (Aelred) to admit that though his friend is often "difficult of temperament", he does show self-restraint and tact to a great extent, within the perimenter of their friendship.

After Aelred has responded to Gratian, Walter quickly interjects a question. Walter's query regarding one's behavior and attitude towards former friends (ill-chosen persons who have succumbed to various vices) evokes a careful, reasoned response from Aelred of Rievaulx. Following Cicero's advice in the

De Amicitia, Aelred suggests that when possible, it is better to "unstitch"[83] rather than "break" or "dissolve" unsuitable affiliation. However, if serious occasions arise, such as danger to one's parent or country through the folly of one's friend, then, of course, "immediate estrangement or separation," is imperative. On the other hand, Aelred's classicism is invariably fused to his Christian faith - a faith that was particularly influenced by the fourth gospel. Consequently, he advises Walter and Gratian:

> "He that is a friend loves at all times."[84] If the one whom you love offends you, continue to love him despite the hurt. His conduct may compel the withdrawal of friendship but never of love. Be concerned as much as you can for his welfare, safeguard his reputation, and never betray the secrets of his friendship, even though he should betray yours.[85]

Walter's need for specific instructions leads him to question Aelred very closely:

> What are these faults, pray, for which you say friendship should be dissolved little by little?[86]

Aelred mentions the five, previously cited, faults which are inimical to friendship and adds a sixth (characteristic of his sense of pastoral duty) - harm done to those for whom one is responsible. In order to illustrate his conviction that "love ought not to outweigh religion, or faith, or charity towards one's neighbor, or the welfare of the people," Aelred draws upon examples from the Bible. As usual, he concludes his advice to Walter and Gratian with a counterpoint - a juxtaposition of classical and Christian perspectives:

> For when friendship has made of two one, just as that which is one cannot be divided, so also friendship cannot be separated from itself. Therefore it is evident that a friendship, which permits of division, was never, in the respect in which it is injured, a true friendship at all, because "friendship which can end, was never true friendship."[87]

True to his commitment to <u>caritas</u> and his innate commonsense, Aelred suggests that

> Four elements in particular seem to pertain to friendship: namely, love and affection, security and happiness.[88]

He advises Walter and Gratian that any of the six reasons previously mentioned must compel one to withdraw "affection, security and happiness" from interchanges with the former friend. According to Aelred, trust and delight, ease and emotional security cannot really exist or be extended to a former friend. However,

> love should not be withdrawn; yet all this should be done from a certain moderation and reverence, so that, if there has not been too great a shock, some traces of the former friendship always seem to remain.[89]

Walter with his keen, inquiring intellect, insists on a summary of Aelred's advice on <u>Spiritual Friendship</u>. Aelred's "brief recapitulation"[90] indicates his ability to be succinct when he so chose.

Aelred has preserved for posterity some of the colloquial asides of Walter and Gratian. He has presented (without condemnation or rancor) their all-too-human foibles and fears in vivid vignettes in the final section of <u>Spiritual Friendship</u>.

In spite of his seriousness towards his vocation, Aelred had too keen a relish for what was humorous and human, to "whitewash" in his work the follies of Gratian and Walter. Aelred has also recorded the coltish, schoolboyish quality of their comments - a reluctance to countenance "intruders" during their tête-à-têtes and their somewhat "cheeky", judgemental opinion of "the others." Their interchange is recorded by Aelred.

> Walter: This is truly opportune for I have my eye glued on the door for fear that someone will break in who will either put an end to our delights, or mingle some bitterness therewith, or introduce something trivial.
>
> Gratian: The cellarer is coming; if you grant him admitance, you will have no opportunity of proceeding further. But see, I am guarding the door; do, Father go on as you have begun.[91]

After this interlude, Aelred's discourse on spiritual friendship continues in a grave, dignified and sincere manner. He instructs them that:

> There are four qualities which must be tested in a friend: loyalty, right intention, discretion and patience.[92]

"Right intention" in the sense that the friend must expect nothing from this affiliation except "God and its natural good." Discretion in friendship, according to Aelred, involves comprehension of responsibilities towards one's friend - responsibilities which include occasional, necessary correction. Aelred's concept of a friend's patience has both an abbatial and a Cistercian quality to it.

Aelred also extols loyalty, praising it as "the nurse and guardian" of spiritual friendship. Moreover, he regards misfortune as the best touchstone of fidelity in friendship and cites a proverb from the Hebrew Bible in favor of his thesis ("He that is a friend loves at all times, and a brother is proved in distress." Prov. 17:17).

Aelred also counsels Walter and Gratian to test the loyalty and discretion of their friends by initially trusting them with minor secrets before entrusting them with "profound secrets." Furthermore, Aelred suggests that only a friend who has proved himself impervious to the seduction of malicious rumors, suspicions and doubts and has clearly demonstrated (over a span of time) his loyalty and stability of character, should be trusted.

Again, Aelred interrupts the lofty tone of his discourse on spiritual friendship by comments from Gratian which provide us with some hitherto unknown facts about the abbot of Rievaulx.

> Just now I call to mind that friend of yours across the sea, whom you have often mentioned to us, the one whom you proved the truest and most faithful friend... When certain individuals bore false witness against you, he not only did not relinquish his faith in you, but was not moved by any hesitation whatsoever; something you could not presume upon even from your dearest friend, the old sacristan of Clairvaux.[93]

This speech also reveals to us the identity of Aelred's "dearest friend" - i.e. "the old sacristan of Clairvaux." Dubois believes that this person was Gerard, the brother of Bernard of Clairvaux.

Aelred characteristically relies upon Cicero's De Amicitia, as well as the New Testament and the works of the Church Fathers to emphasize his conviction that there must be no expectations of material gain or hope of worldly advancement from a friend, who must indeed be loved as oneself and to whom one should be linked only by a mutual love of God. Aelred again reiterates his conviction that

> friendships among the poor are generally more secure than among the rich, since poverty takes away the hope of gain in such a way as not to decrease the love of friendship but rather to increase it.[94]

Aelred follows Cicero's example (in De Amicitia) by rebuking those who adhere to a "double standard" in friendship - people who "wish a friend to be in character what they themselves cannot be."[95] Although Aelred strongly advocated discretion in the choice of a friend and moderation and balance in "proceeding gradually in affection" - his counsel is neither tepid nor uncharitable. He exhorts Gratian and Walter not to be hasty in withdrawing their affection, if initially disappointed by a friend, and to be unflagging in their care and concern for their friends

> ...let no one in choosing or testing friends weary of being solicitous, since the fruit of this labor is the medicine of life and the most solid foundation of immortality.[96]

Again Aelred follows Cicero's example by informing Walter that "without friends absolutely no life can be happy."[97] Walter is still not convinced, preferring the stoical concept that one's life is safer, hence happier, without the cares and concerns of friendship. To disprove Walter's theory, Aelred cites Cicero's analogy of imagining oneself as the sole survivor of the human race, in solitary possession of the earth. Walter is forced to admit that without a friend or in the company of a stranger, one cannot even enjoy great prosperity.

Aelred's abundant optimism expresses itself in his concept of the afterlife. He admits that while on earth, prudence and practicality coerce one to exercise judicious selection and probation of friends. However, Aelred's naturally warm and inclusive nature probably chafed under the necessary restraints of prudence. Consequently, he envisions a universal, symphonic afterlife where

> ...the happiness of each one individually is the happiness of all, and the universality of all happiness is the possession of each individual. There one finds no hiding of thoughts, no dissembling of affection. This is true and eternal friendship, which begins in this life and is perfected in the next, which here belongs to the few where few are good, but there belongs to all where all are good. Here, probation is necessary since there is a mingling of wise and unwise; there they need no probation...[98]

Aelred's comments enable Walter to come to the conclusion that every person wishes to be loved and that one is "happier in proportion" to the number of friends in one's life.

Aelred then provides us with a glimpse of the Rievaulx community during his abbacy. In spite of occasional dissenters and some encounters with eccentric persons, by and large, there was a well-knit, harmonious atmosphere in Rievaulx, generated (contemporary sources inform us) to a large extent, by his empathetic leadership.

> The day before yesterday, as I was walking the round of the cloister of the monastery, the brethren were sitting around forming as it were a most loving crown... In that multitude of brethren I found no one whom I did not love, and no one by whom, I felt sure, I was not loved. I was filled with such joy that it surpassed all the delights of this world. I felt, indeed, my spirit transfused into all and the affection of all to have passed into me, so that I could say..."Behold, how good and how pleasant it is for brethren to dwell together in unity."[99]

In response to Gratian's question whether Aelred has taken everyone he loves into his confidence, Aelred reminds him that this would be imprudent and inappropriate, since

> We embrace very many with every affection, and yet in such a way that we do not admit them to the secrets of friendship, which consists especially in the revelation of all our confidences and plans...How many, therefore, so we love before whom it would be imprudent to lay bare our souls and pour out our inner hearts! Men whose age or feeling or discretion is not sufficient to bear such revelations.[100]

Walter finds Aelred's definition of spiritual friendship beyond his reach ("This friendship is so sublime and perfect that I dare not aspire to it"), preferring Augustine's descriptions of his youthful affiliations in his <u>Confessions</u>.

In his reasonable manner, Aelred concedes that there is something to be said for the youthful camaraderie (between Augustine and his friends) that Augustine describes in his <u>Confessions</u>. However, Aelred does not want Walter to regard this camaraderie as the zenith of spiritual friendship but, rather, as its initial stage.

Aelred goes on to reiterate and comment on the qualities that are essential for the flowering of spiritual friendship. He states that

> Loyalty, then, is the foundation of stability and constancy in friendship, for nothing is stable that is unfaithful.[101]

Aelred also exhorts Walter to avoid suspicion and uncharitable thoughts about one's friends, suggesting the addition of

> affability in speech, cheerfulness of countenance, suavity in manners, serenity in the expression of the eyes, matters in which there is to be found no slight relish to friendship.[102]

Aelred is quick to indicate that he is not referring to "levity and dissipation" but to a fluency of accord.

> For sadness and a rather severe demeanor give one a certain appearance of gravity, but friendship aught to be, so to speak, rather relaxed at times; it aught to be somewhat free and mild, and rather incline to congeniality and easiness of approach...[103]

Again following the injunctions of both Cicero[104] and Jerome,[105] Aelred states that

> It is also a law of friendship that a superior must be on a plane of equality with the inferior...Therefore, in friendship, which is the perfect gift of nature and grace alike, let the lofty descend, the lowly ascend; the rich be in want, the poor become rich; and thus let each communicate his condition to the other, so that equality may be the result... Never, therefore, prefer yourself to your friend; but if you find yourself the superior in those things which we have mentioned, then do not hesitate to abase yourself before your friend, to give him your confidence,

> to praise him if he is shy, and to confer honor
> upon him in inverse proportion to that warranted
> by his lowliness and poverty.106

Again, Aelred cites the loyalty, selflessness and nobility of Jonathan's exemplary affection for David, as the paradigm of spiritual friendship.

Aelred now turns his attention to illustrating to his students the importance of "the question of how the benefits of friendship are to be cultivated."107 Aelred as usual refers to both Cicero's De Amicitia and the Bible, citing Boaz as an example of a considerate benefactor. His advice is both pithy and pertinent - apt even today.

> Therefore, give to your friend in such a way that you
> do not reproach him, or expect a reward. Do not wrinkle
> your brow, or turn aside your countenance or avert
> your eyes; but with a serene countenance, a cheerful
> aspect and pleasing speech, anticipate the request
> of him who is seeking a favor. Meet him with kindness,
> so that you may appear to be granting his request with-
> out being asked. The sensitive soul thinks of nothing
> more worthy of a blush than to beg...anticipate...re-
> quests by good services,...so that the recipient, rather
> than the giver, appears to be bestowing the favor.108

Walter then asks how people in religious life "who are permitted to receive nothing and to bestow nothing" are to experience "the charm of spiritual friendship?"109 Aelred's advice to Walter reminds one of the closing section of his "Rule for a Recluse." Aelred expresses his belief that it is a blessing to be free of the cares of "carnal" gift-giving and receiving, and indicates to Walter the

> resources in spiritual love, by means of which friends
> can be of aid and advantage to one another. The first

is to be solicitous for one another, to pray for one
another, to blush for one another, to rejoice for one
another, to grieve for one another's fall as one's
own, to regard one another's progress as one's own.[110]

In keeping with his own pastoral temperament and abbatial vocation, Aelred pleads with Walter and Gratian to aid those in need

> By whatever means are in one's power, one ought to
> raise the weak, support the infirm, console the
> afflicted, restrain the wrathful.[111]

He also emphasizes the salutary effect of the presence of friends which prevents one from behaving in an indecorous of dishonorable manner and states unequivocally that

> the best companion of friendship is reverence, and
> so he who deprives friendship of respect takes away
> its greatest adornment.[112]

Contrary to Walter's hagiographical determination (in *Vita Aelredi*) to depict his abbot as a paragon of virtue, Aelred gives his readers some interesting vignettes of his own shortcomings in this section of his *Spiritual Friendship*.

> How often has the nod of my friend restrained or
> extinguished the flame of anger aroused within me
> and already bursting forth into public gaze! How
> frequently his rather severe demeanor has repressed
> the unbecoming word already on my lips! How often
> when carelessly breaking into laughter, or lapsing
> into idleness I have recovered a proper dignity at
> his approach.[113]

Aelred also emphasizes a friend's responsibility not only to provide counsel, empathy and appreciation, but, whenever necessary, admonition as well. He advises Walter and Gratian not to fall into the trap of acrimony - venting "outsurging rage" and bitterness under the guise of solicitude, for "among friends there is no excuse for this vice."[114] His counsel is that "a friend ought to...correct...humbly and sympathetically."[115] True to his intuitive insight into human nature, and acceptance of the diversity of temperaments - Aelred suggests that one "ought even to study the disposition" of his friend's "heart."[116]

> For there are those with whom coaxings are effective, and such persons quite readily assent thereto. There are others who are impervious to coaxing, and are more easily corrected by a word or blow. Let a man, therefore, conform and adapt himself to his friend to be in harmony with his disposition.[117]

Quoting from classical, as well as Christian works, Aelred emphasizes the importance of truthful communication between friends and the avoidance of hypocrisy:

> Accordingly, let there be no hesitation among friends and no pretense, a thing most of all repugnant to friendship. Indeed, a man owes truth to his friend, without which the name of friendship has no value.[118]

However, Aelred concludes this speech on an ambiguous note:

> Therefore, friendship ought so to be cultivated that, although it may perhaps tolerate dissimulation for good reasons, it will never tolerate simulation.[119]

At Walter's insistence, he clarifies this point, describing simulation as "a kind of deceptive agreement, opposed to the judgement of reason"[120] and dissimulation as "dispensing with, or a putting off of punishment or correction, without interior approval, in consideration of place, time, or person."[121] Consistent with his humane temperament, Aelred advocates discretion when correcting any erring person, particularly a friend, and advises that careful consideration be given to the inner condition and external circumstances of the culprit.

> For if a friend when he is in the midst of others should commit some fault, he should not suddenly and publicly be reproached; but one ought to "dissemble" because of the place, nay, further, as far as is compatible with truth, one ought to excuse what he has done, and wait to administer in secret the deserved rebuke. Likewise, at a time when the mind is engrossed in many considerations and so is less receptive of those matters which must be spoken, or, when, for other reasons that have intervened, the friend's feelings are a trifle more moved and he is, in consequence, somewhat disturbed - in both instances there is need of dissimulation until the tumult within has been calmed and he can endure the needful correction.[122]

Pleased with Aelred's explanation, Walter then inquires whether one who is in a position to offer "honors and distinctions" should confer them on a friend or not. Aelred's advice shows the cool prudence that was such a balanced counterpoint to his affective nature:

> For there are some persons who think they are not loved because they cannot be promoted, and who allege that they are despised, if they are not entrusted with responsibilities and offices...Thus great caution must be observed in the conferring of dignities and offices, especially ecclesiastical ones. You should not be concerned about what you are able to bestow, but rather about what he, upon whom you bestow anything, can endure.[123]

In keeping with his predilection for balanced counsel, Aelred presents his conviction:

> Let us afford our friend whatever love, whatever sweetness, whatever charity we can; but let us impose vain honors and

> burdens on those who, reason dictates, should be
> burdened, realizing that a man never truly loves a
> friend if he is not satisfied with his friend as he
> is, but must needs add these worthless and contemptible
> honors.
>
> One must also greatly guard against permitting a too
> tender affection from hindering greater utility. This
> would be the case were we unwilling to part from or
> to burden those whom we embrace in greater charity
> when great hope of more abundant fruit is to be realized.
> For this is well-ordered friendship, namely, that reason
> rules affection, and that we attend more to the general
> welfare than to our friend's good humor.[124]

To illustrate and substantiate the above-mentioned comments, Aelred provides us with another rare glimpse of his personal life, in the description of his rapport with two cherished friends whom scholars have identified as Simon and Geoffrey (of Dinant).[125] Simon who died when they were both young was a chosen but untested friend. Geoffrey, on the other hand, was a life long colleague whom Aelred movingly describes as

> devoted to me from boyhood even to middle age, and
> loved by me, mounted with through all the stages of
> friendship, as far as human imperfection permitted.[126]

Aelred informs us that it was his admiration for Geoffrey's virtues which first evoked his affection for him. After observing this loyal, selfless man for decades and being certain that "he had advanced far in the life of virtue and grace," Aelred "consulted the brethren and imposed upon him the burden of subpriorship." Aelred has described towards the end of *Spiritual Friendship* the tests of loyalty and discretion which he and Geoffrey posed to one another and which they both passed, so that without endangering one another's spiritual growth, they became each other's "most cherished of friends." Aelred concludes his recollection of this friendship, almost on a rhapsodic tone:

> What more is there, then, that I can say? Was it not a foretaste of blessedness thus to love and thus to be loved; thus to help and thus to be helped; and in this way from the sweetness of fraternal charity to wing one's flight aloft to that more sublime splendor of divine love, and by that ladder of charity now to mount to the love of Christ himself; and again to descend to the love of neighbor, there pleasantly to rest? And so, in this friendship of ours, which we have introduced by way of example, if you see ought worthy of imitation, profit by it to advance your own perfection.[127]

The last three pages of Aelred's Spiritual Friendship is a masterly synopsis[128] of the entire book. He includes in this summary the importance of prayer - particularly the power of a friend's prayer which is

> the more efficacious in proportion as it is more lovingly sent to God, with tears which either fear excites or affection awakens or sorrow evokes.[129]

Aelred believed that the friend though engaged in unselfish prayer, is richly rewarded by greater spiritual insight and inner closeness to the Christian goal.

> Thus ascending to that holy love with which he embraces a friend to that with which he embraces Christ, he will joyfully partake in abundance of the spiritual fruit of friendship, awaiting the fullness of all things in the life to come.[130]

Aelred concludes his Spiritual Friendship on a note of abundant optimism, delineating what he believed to be the fruition of spiritual friendship - a harvest which includes all beings in the epiphany and fullness of unalloyed awareness of the Divine Reality.

> Then, with the dispelling of all anxiety by reason of which we now fear and are solicitous for one another, with the removal of all adversity with which it now behooves us to bear for one another, and, above all, with the destruction of the sting of death together with death itself, whose pangs now often trouble us and force us to grieve for one another, with salvation secured, we shall rejoice in the eternal possession of Supreme Goodness; and this friendship, to which here we admit but few, will be outpoured upon all and be all outpoured upon God, and God shall be all in all.[131]

A SYNOPSIS OF SOURCES AND SOME RESPONSES TO
AELRED'S SPIRITUAL FRIENDSHIP (DE SPIRITUALI AMICITIA)

Aelred of Rievaulx's Spiritual Friendship (De Spirituali Amicitia) was profoundly influenced by Cicero's De Amicitia which, in turn, shows marked indebtedness to Aristotle's Nichomachean Ethics, Books VIII and IX.[132]

Charles Dumont in his otherwise interesting essay on Aelred's Spiritual Friendship was disconcerted by the influence of Cicero on this work and defensively stated that

> It would be erroneous, and indeed a great mistake, to think of Aelred as clandestinely smuggling profane literature, the De Amicitia of Cicero, into the cloister under the cloak of piety. Such a compromising attitude would be completely contrary to the Cistercians' spirit of authenticity and loyalty.[133]

However, J. Dubois,[134] A. Squire,[135] Odo Brooke[136] and Douglas Roby[137] all acknowledge Aelred's considerable debt to Cicero. Squire, one of the foremost Aelredian scholars of this century, informs us that

> ...in no other adaptation of Cicero's teaching does so much of this source survive.[138]

While Roby observes that

There is hardly a page on which some quotation or at least some allusion to the De Amicitia does not appear. It is estimated that fully one-third of Cicero's work is contained in Aelred's...However, though Aelred took Cicero for his master in the matter and even in the outline of the Spiritual Friendship, he did not hesitate to adapt him when he was insufficiently Christian and even to differ with him on some points.[139]

The other important sources of Aelred's Spiritual Friendship are the Hebrew Bible, the New Testament, and the works of the Fathers. To Aelred, the friendship of David and Jonathan became the paradigm of spiritual friendship. Aelred also alludes to the book of Proverbs and the Song of Songs in his Spiritual Friendship. The Gospel according to St. John[140] in the New Testament, deeply influenced Aelred's life and work. Consequently, it is not surprising that there are references to this gospel throughout the tapestry of his Spiritual Friendship.

The influence of Augustine's Confessions is also discernible in Aelred's Spiritual Friendship. However, Aelred's independence (as an author and as a person) is clearly evident in this book. Douglas Roby's comments are relevant in this context. He states that Aelred's Spiritual Friendship is

> ...no more a florilegium of the Fathers than it is a copy of Cicero.
>
> ...But perhaps even more striking than Aelred's confident reworking of his sources is his independent sympathy with the humanistic tradition...The north of Britain, too, had its own tradition of learning and played a noble rôle in the preservation of the classics during the dark days of the barbarian invasions; especially in Durham that tradition had never been forgotten. Aelred was very much a part of that tradition of classical education, and it was a happy fusion of his own personal needs and the opportunities of this tradition which enabled him to create the Classical-Christian humanism of the Spiritual Friendship.[141]

As noted above, Aelred's Spiritual Friendship is not an uneasy amalgam of disparate sources but a harmonious synthesis.

Gracious, genial by temperament, Aelred appreciated and applauded the intrinsic beauty and dignity of human kind.[142] To live without friends, under the guise of safeguarding one's self from possible sorrow, was abhorrent to him. When Walter Daniel suggested this possibility in Book II of *Spiritual Friendship*, Aelred responded with uncharacteristic indignation:

> Paul must have been a fool, for he was unwilling to live without care and solicitude for others...
> ...I would say those men are beasts rather than human beings who declare that a man ought to live in such a way as to be to no one a source of consolation, to no one a source even of grief or burden; to take no delight in the good fortune of another, or impart to others no bitterness because of their own misfortune, caring to cherish no one and to be cherished by no one. Heaven forbid that they truly love anyone who think of friendship as a trade; for such with their lips only declare themselves friends when the hope of some temporal advantage favors them or when they try to make their friend an accomplice in some base deed.[143]

For Aelred friendship was not even an expedient stair by which one ascended to the Divine Presence. Charles Dumont perceptively indicates that

> ...The experience of friendship for Aelred is a means of perfection, indeed only a degree short of perfection. From being a friend of a man, one becomes the friend of God...Perfect union of two wills: this definition given by Cicero and Sallust is brought up when these two classical authors are discussed in the first dialogue. Love of God is essentially the union of a human will with the will of God...[144]

Although Aelred's responsibilities as an abbot and a counsellor necessitated prudent advice about the cautious choice and selection of suitable friends, his inherently inclusive nature sought solace in a radiant concept of the afterlife - a realm where friendship can be freely accorded to all.[145]

Although Adele Fiske has written an authoritative book called Friends and Friendship in the Monastic Tradition[146] which provides one with many valuable insights, recent historical research indicates that

> In spite of Mother Fiske's industry, however,...this positive valuation of human friendship was relatively unusual, and...the tradition of the Fathers and of the monastic authors of the early middle ages was very reserved in its appreciation of the value of friendship...[147]
> ...the earliest monastic authors had been ambivalent about the value of particular friendships in the monastic community...The dangers to the spiritual life of pseudo-friendships, leading to factions and the danger of sexual temptation, had led most authors to stress the exclusive desire for God at the expense of the emotional satisfactions of love of neighbors and friends. Thus when Cassian treated the subject of personal friendships in the Conferences the weight of the discussion fell on avoiding anger and distraction from the purity of the love of God, rather than on the spiritual advantages of love between brothers.
>
> The literature of the Carolingen revival of religious life is equally focused away from the particular friendship of the cloister...the emphasis is on a rather conventional and formal friendship, imitated from late Roman models of politeness, rather than a true and deeply felt intimacy...[148]

It was not until the late eleventh century that spiritual friendship was reawakened in monastic circles through the influence of Anselm of Bec whose moving letters and "Prayer for friends" indicate that the future Archbishop of Canterbury "developed a spirituality of friendship as an aspect of pursuit of God."[149]

In the twelfth century, Bernard of Clairvaux and William of St. Thierry[150] not only penned glowing sermons based on their understanding and exegesis of the "Song of Songs" but wrote vividly on the subject of spiritual friendship, as well. Moreover, in the secular world of the twelfth century, France gave birth to the poetry of the trouvères and troubadors who extolled fervor, friendship and hidden, chivalrous love for the ladies of their choice. The influence of courtly love poetry did not remain confined to France. A famous patroness of poets and musicians, Eleanor, was not only the Duchess of Acquitaine but also the Queen of England. Consequently, she helped to widen the sphere of chivalry and courtly literature.

Although Aelred's Spiritual Friendship should be considered in its historic context, there is a classical restraint[151] (which is absent in Walter Daniel's Vita Ailredi, for example), an absence of effusiveness in his warm, yet balanced analysis and assessment of spiritual friendship.

Douglas Roby informs us that Aelred's Spiritual Friendship "inspired no successors in the monastic tradition."[152] However, scribes had a penchant for this work. Several copies of this book still exist in France, England, Spain and "the Low Countries." Moreover, four abbreviated versions of Aelred's Spiritual Friendship were extant in the fourteenth century. One of these versions was attributed to St. Augustine and the other to an English Austin Friar of the thirteenth century called Thomas of Frakaham.

In the thirteenth century Peter of Blois produced his
Christian Friendship - a book which is a purloined amalgam
of Aelred's Mirror of Charity and Spiritual Friendship.
Peter of Blois' Christian Friendship which scholars regard
as a "full-scale plagiarism" of Aelred's work was, in turn,
attributed to Cassiodorus. Furthermore, Jean de Meun, the
author of Romance of the Rose attempted a partial translation
of Aelred's Spiritual Friendship.

After the fourteenth century, "traces of Aelred's influence
are lost to our view."[153]

> The late middle ages and the counter-reformation shared
> a distrust of the "particular friendship"...As modern
> moral theology has turned away from the abstract and
> defensive attitude of handbook scholasticism...there
> has been a revival of interest in Aelred and the
> Spiritual Friendship.[154]

After being neglected for six centuries, Aelred's
Spiritual Friendship is now under frequent,[155] occasionally
anachronistic, scrutiny. In recent times, perhaps the most
cogent evaluation of Aelred's Spiritual Friendship was penned
by Thomas Merton in his introduction to Hallier's The Monastic
Theology of Aelred of Rievaulx.

> The thing that is most characteristic of Aelred's monastic
> theology is its emphasis on friendship. His doctrine is
> not simply a theology of community but a theology of
> friendship. The Christian life is, for Aelred, simply
> the full flowering of freedom and consent in the perfec-
> tion of friendship. Friendship with other human beings
> as a epiphany of friendship with God. In this, surely
> he is quite modern. "To live without friends," he says,
> "is to live like a beast..."

...For Aelred, the monastic community life is simply a life of friendship. The monastic life is an education in friendship...it is a sharing in the friendship of God...For this very reason - we must dare to admit it - he was for a long time regarded as "dangerous" in certain monasteries. Not so long ago, some of Aelred's books were kept under lock and key in Trappist libraries - just as John of the Cross was kept locked up in some Carmels.[156]

1. See Douglas Roby's "Sources of the Spiritual Friendship" in his introduction to Aelred's Spiritual Friendship (Kalamazoo, Michigan: Cistercian Publications, 1977), p. 31.

2. Aelred, Spiritual Friendship, p. 45.

3. Ibid., pp. 46-47.

4. See E. Gilson, The Mystical Theology of St. Bernard, tr. A. Downes (New York: Sheed and Ward, 1940), p. 7.

   Also, see Odo Brooke's "Monastic Theology and St. Aelred" in his Studies in Monastic Theology (Kalamazoo, Michigan: Cistercian Publications, 1980), p. 222.

5. Amédée Hallier, The Monastic Theology of Aelred of Rievaulx, tr. C. Heaney (Shannon, Ireland: Irish University Press, 1969).

6. See Aelred's Mirror of Charity, pp. 64, 76.

7. Aelred, Spiritual Friendship, p. 47.

8. Ibid., p. 51.

9. Marcus Tullius Cicero, "On Friendship", Tr. W. Falconer in De Senectute - De Amicitia - De Divinatione (New York: Putnam, 1922), pp. 130-131.

10. Aelred, Spiritual Friendship, p. 54.

11. Ibid., pp. 54-55.

12. Ibid., p. 58.

13. Ibid., p. 59.

14. See Douglas Roby's introduction to Aelred's Spiritual Friendship, pp. 22-24, 29-30.

    Also see A. Squire, Aelred of Rievaulx..., pp. 100-101.

15. Cicero, De Amicitia, p. 139.

16. Psalms 15:2. Genesis 2:18, 2:21f.

17. See Bernard of Clairvaux, "On the Song of Songs," Sermon 59:2.

18. Aelred, Spiritual Friendship, p. 63.

19. *Ibid.*, p. 65.

20. *Ibid.*, p. 66.

21. See Douglas Roby's introduction to Aelred's *Spiritual Friendship*, p. 14.

22. Aelred, *Spiritual Friendship*, p. 66.

23. *Ibid.*, p. 69.

24. *Ibid.*

25. *Ibid.*

26. *Ibid.*

27. See Walther, *Prouerbia Sententiaque Latinitatis Medii Aeui*, Vol. I (Gottingen, 1936), p. 356.

    Xenophon uses this proverb in *Memorables*, 1, 3, 5.

28. Aelred, *Spiritual Friendship*, p. 70.

29. *Ibid.*

30. *Ibid.*, pp. 70-71.

31. *Ibid.*, p. 71.

32. *Ibid.*

33. Eccles. 4:10. See also St. Ambrose, *Duties of the Clergy*, p. 88.

34. Aelred, *Spiritual Friendship*, pp. 71-72.

35. *Ibid.*, p. 73.

36. *Ibid.*

37. See 2 Cor. 13. See A. Hallier, *The Monastic Theology of Aelred of Rievaulx*, pp. 89-98.

38. Cicero, *De Amicitia*, p. 139.

39. Aelred, *Spiritual Friendship*, p. 74.

40. *Ibid.*

41. *Ibid.*, pp. 74-75.

42. *Ibid.*, p. 76.

43. *Ibid.*

44. See A. Louth's discussion of "the Greek word <u>nous</u> and its derivatives" in <u>The Origins of the Christian Mystical Tradition</u> (Oxford: Clarendon Press, 1981) pp. xv-xvii.

45. Aelred, <u>Spiritual Friendship</u>, p. 77.

46. *Ibid.*

47. *Ibid.*

48. Jn. 15:13.

49. Aelred, <u>Spiritual Friendship</u>, p. 78.

50. *Ibid.*, pp. 78-79.

51. Cicero, <u>De Amicitia</u>, pp. 127-128, 150-151.

52. Gen. 3:6. 1 Sam. 22:17f. 2 Sam. 13:3f. 2 Sam. 15:12f.

53. Aelred, <u>Spiritual Friendship</u>, pp. 79-80. Aelred refers to the claims of Octavian Maledetti (who called himself Pope Victor IV) against Alexander III who was regarded as the true pope.

54. *Ibid.*, p. 80.

55. *Ibid.*, p. 81.

56. *Ibid.*, pp. 81-82.

57. *Ibid.*, p. 82.

58. *Ibid.*, p. 83.

59. *Ibid.*

60. *Ibid.*, p. 84.

61. *Ibid.*

62. See Odo Brooke's "Monastic Theory and St. Aelred" in <u>Studies in Monasticism</u>, p. 223.

63. Aelred, <u>Spiritual Friendship</u>, p. 85.

64. *Ibid.*, p. 87.

65. *Ibid.*

66. *Ibid.*

67. *Ibid.*, p. 91.

68. *Ibid.*

69. *Ibid.*

70. *Ibid.*, p. 92.

71. *Ibid.*.

72. *Ibid.*

73. *Ibid.*, p. 93.

74. *Ibid.*, p. 94.

75. *Ibid.*

76. *Ibid.*, p. 95.

77. *Ibid.*

78. *Ibid.*, p. 96.

79. *Ibid.* Also see note 15 on p. 96, of Aelred's *Spiritual Friendship*.

80. *Ibid.*, p. 99. See note 28 on p. 99, of Aelred's *Spiritual Friendship*.

81. *Ibid.*

82. *Ibid.*

83. Cato's maxim quoted by Cicero in *De Amicitia*, p. 185.

84. Proverbs 17:17.

85. Aelred, *Spiritual Friendship*, p. 102.

86. *Ibid.*

87. *Ibid.*, p. 103. See note 42 on p. 103, of Aelred's *Spiritual Friendship*.

88. *Ibid.*, p. 103.

89. *Ibid.*

90. *Ibid*., pp. 104-105.

91. *Ibid*., p. 105.

92. *Ibid*.

93. *Ibid*., p. 107.

94. *Ibid*., p. 108.

95. *Ibid*.

96. *Ibid*., 109. Also see note 60, p. 109, of *Spiritual Friendship*.

97. *Ibid*., p. 110. Also see note 63, p. 110, of *Spiritual Friendship*.

98. *Ibid*., p. 111.

99. *Ibid*., p. 112. Also see note 70, p. 112, of *Spiritual Friendship*.

100. *Ibid*., pp. 112-113.

101. *Ibid*., p. 114.

102. *Ibid*.

103. *Ibid*. Also see note 81, p. 114, of *Spiritual Friendship*.

104. Cicero, *De Amicitia*, p. 179.

105. See note 82, p. 115 of Aelred's *Spiritual Friendship*.

106. Aelred, *Spiritual Friendship*, p. 115. Also see note 84, p. 115, of *Spiritual Friendship*.

107. *Ibid*., p. 117.

108. *Ibid*., pp. 118-119.

109. *Ibid*., p. 119.

110. *Ibid*. Also see Aelred's "Rule of Life for a Recluse" in *Treatises and the Pastoral Prayer* (Kalamazoo, Michigan: Cistercian Publications, 1971), pp. 77-78.

111. *Ibid*., p. 78.

112. *Ibid*., p. 120. Also see note 107, p. 120, of *Spiritual Friendship*.

113. *Ibid.*

114. *Ibid.*, p. 121.

115. *Ibid.*

116. *Ibid.*

117. *Ibid.*, pp. 121-122.

118. *Ibid.*, p. 122.

119. *Ibid.*

120. *Ibid.*, p. 123.

121. *Ibid.*

122. *Ibid.*

123. *Ibid.*, p. 124.

124. *Ibid.*, pp. 125-126.

125. See Powicke's introduction to *Vita Aelredi*, p. lxvi.

126. Aelred, *Spiritual Friendship*, p. 127.

127. *Ibid.*, p. 129.

128. *Ibid.*, pp. 130-132.

129. *Ibid.*, p. 131.

130. *Ibid.*

131. *Ibid.*, pp. 131-132.

132. See Douglas Roby's introduction to *Spiritual Friendship*, p. 30.

133. See C. Dumont's essay on *Spiritual Friendship* in *Cistercian Ideals and Reality*, ed. John R. Sommerfeldt (Kalamazoo, Michigan: 1978), p. 187.

134. J. Dubois, ed., L'amitié spirituelle, Latin text, French translation (Bruges: C. Beyaert, 1948), p. li.

135. A. Squire, Aelred of Rievaulx..., pp. 100-110.

136. Odo Brooke, "Monastic Theology and St. Aelred "in Studies in Monasticism (Kalamazoo, Michigan: Cistercian Publications, 1980), p. 222.

137. See Douglas Roby's introduction to Spiritual Friendship, pp. 22-24, 29-30.

138. A. Squire, Aelred of Rievaulx..., p. 100.

139. See Roby's introduction to Spiritual Friendship, pp. 29-30.

140. See Walter Daniel, Vita Ailredi, p. 58.

141. See Roby's introduction to Spiritual Friendship, pp. 33-34.

142. Aelred, Mirror of Charity, p. 3, 11.

143. Aelred, Spiritual Friendship, pp. 82-83.

144. See Dumont's essay on Spiritual Friendship in Cistercian Ideals and Reality, pp. 193-194.

145. See Aelred, Spiritual Friendship, pp. 131-132.

146. Adele Fiske, Friends and Friendship in the Monastic Tradition (Cuernavaca: CIDOC, 1970), chapters 16 and 18.

147. Both Dumont and Roby have a very myopic reading of St. Augustine's concepts of the love of self, neighbor and of God. Moreover, their misunderstanding of St. Augustine's view of spiritual friendship has led them to attribute to Aelred an originality of concept that is historically inaccurate and which Aelred would have been quick to disclaim. For a cogent, insightful and lucid analysis of some important Augustinian perspectives see Margaret Miles's "Vision: The Eye of the Body and the Eye of the Mind in Saint Augustine's De Trinitate and Confessions" in The Journal of Religion, Vol. 63, No. 2, April, 1982.

148. See Roby's introduction to Spiritual Friendship, p. 15, pp. 36-37.

149. Ibid., p. 37. Also see Southern, *Medieval Humanism...*, p. 33.

150. See Fiske, *Friends...*, pp. 16/1-17/23.

151. See Roby's introduction to *Spiritual Friendship*, p. 34.

152. *Ibid.*, p. 38.

153. *Ibid.*, p. 40.

154. *Ibid.*

155. See the bibliography.

156. See Thomas Merton's introduction to Hallier's *The Monastic Theology of Aelred of Rievaulx*, pp. xi-xii.

CHAPTER IX

"RULE OF LIFE FOR A RECLUSE"
("DE INSTITUTIONE INCLUSARUM")

"Rule of Life for a Recluse" ("De Institutione Inclusarum") was written by Aelred at his sister's request during the closing years of his life. Scholars disagree about the precise date of this work. Squire[1] suggests that it was written during c. 1163-4, while Knowles[2] regards it as a slightly earlier work, composed during c. 1160-2.

The "Rule for a Recluse" though understandably influenced by the Rule of Benedict and some of the Church Fathers,[3] is, nevertheless, original in several ways. Thanks to this work, we discover vivid vignettes[4] of indiscreet behavior among those professing a religious vocation, moving autobiographical excerpts[5] in which Aelred shares with his sibling his own struggles and inspirations, as well as a symphonic conclusion which anticipates Dante's Divine Comedy.

Nothing is known of Aelred's sister except the fact that she was an anchoress of excellent reputation. It may be pertinent to add that "anchorholds"[6] were a fairly common feature of the north English landscape during the Middle Ages.

Aelred's "Rule for a Recluse" has a distinguished place[7] both in the literary, as well as in the ecclesiastical works of medieval England. Although written in Latin, his hilarious, deft sketches of deviant and self-indulgent behavior among so-called "religious" people anticipate Chaucer's robust humor and exposure of "clerics" in The Canterbury Tales.[8]

From a historical viewpoint, this work stands in the tradition of books and letters which were written to provide specific guidance to those who had a genuinely contemplative vocation. It is possible that Aelred was cognizant of Jerome's[9] letter (advising virginity) to Eustochium, as well as the ninth century Rule for Solitaries by Grimlac.[10] Moreover, several modern scholars[11] of the medieval period think that Aelred's "Rule for a Recluse", written in the twelfth century, influenced the fourteenth century spiritual classic Ancrene Riwle. Internal evidence indicates that the author of The Cloud of Unknowing was also influenced by some of Aelred's works.[12]

The first section of the "Rule for a Recluse" contains Aelred's detailed injunctions to his sister (and the young women who sought her guidance) regarding the importance of simplicity, silence and chastity for those who had chosen a hermetic life.

In true Cistercian fashion, Aelred advocates the alternation of **manual work and prayer**. He also gives the reader a glimpse of **two aspects of himself which are seldom revealed** in his other works. One does not usually impute this gracious abbot and humanist with a gift for keen satire[13] or for insistent emphasis on a medley of strictures. However, these uncharacteristic facets of Aelred are very much in evidence in this work. One wonders whether the gruesome incidents which coalesced around a Gilbertine nun of Watton[14] (a matter in which Aelred's arbitration was sought) had caused him to impart such surprisingly stringent advice to his sister and those who sought her counsel.

In the second section of this work Aelred exhorts and pleads with those who have chosen a hermetic life to safeguard their chastity. His injunctions may sound somewhat high-pitched and excessive to modern readers. However, it is pertinent to remember that the "Rule for a Recluse" was written specifically for anchoresses, at the insistence of his sister who had embraced the hermetic life.

Aelred's affectionate and essentially democratic nature (in spite of his aristocratic upbringing and his abbatial responsibilities) asserts itself in a moving self-disclosure[15] of his own struggles and his denunciation of various forms of snobbery[16] - pride of lineage, sanctimoniousness, love of luxurious surroundings, etc.

Aelred warns his sister and her students that chastity "although...the flower and adornment of all the virtues,... withers and fades away without humility."[17] In his characteristic way, Aelred emphasizes the centrality of charity (caritas-unconditional love) in one's inner life and consequent actions:

> ...the end of the Law is charity, coming from a pure heart and a good conscience and unfeigned faith.
>
> Let it be in these that you glory and find your happiness; within, not without, in true virtues, not in paintings and statues.[18]

Aelred (as the anonymous author of The Cloud of Unknowing[19] was to do two centuries later) expressed and explained to his sister the service[20] which a contemplative renders to society - simply by the hidden and healing presence of one who is utterly consecrated to the One. Like Mary (the sister of Martha), the contemplative, though not outwardly productive, nevertheless has chosen "the better part" by offering her undivided attention to the presence of God. Though lacking in material possessions, such a person, according to Aelred, is able to be an instrument of inspiration to humanity by her offering of unstinted caritas (in the sense of caring, tenderness, goodwill, altruism) to others. Aelred speaks of this gift in vivid prose:

> Nothing is more valuable, a certain holy man has said, than good will. Let this be your offering. What is more useful than prayer? Let this be your largesse. What is more humane than pity? Let this be your alms. So embrace the whole world with the arms of your love and in that act at once consider and congratulate the good, contemplate and mourn over the wicked. In that act look upon the afflicted and the oppressed and feel compassion for them. In that act call to mind the wretchedness of the poor, the groans of orphans, the

abandonment of widows, the gloom of the sorrowful, the needs of travellers, the prayers of virgins, the perils of those at sea, the temptations of monks, the responsibilities of prelates, the labors of those waging war. In your love taken them all to your heart, weep over them, offer your prayers for them. Such alms are more pleasing to God, more acceptable to Christ, more becoming your profession, more fruitful to those who receive them. The performance of such good works as these help you to live out your profession instead of upsetting you; they increase the love you have for your neighbor instead of diminishing it; they are a safeguard, not an obstacle to tranquility of mind.[21]

Aelred also offered his sister a glimpse of the unitive state that all mystics seek and some momentarily experience:

Let these things serve to increase your charity, not to provide empty show. From all of them you must ascend to unity, for only one thing is necessary. That is the one thing, the unity which is found only in the One, by the One, with the One with whom there is no variation, no shadow of change. The man who unites... with Him becomes one spirit with Him, passing into that unity which is always the same and whose years do not come to an end. This unity is charity, as it were the edge and border of the spiritual vesture.[22]

In spite of conscious echoes from the New Testament, the above excerpt has a distinctly Plotinian flavor. However, the Johannine influence is certainly present. The emphasis on love (*caritas*), as well as on spiritual unity, is reiterated by Aelred in his own distinctive way:

Indeed the nuptial robe, woven out of all the array of the virtues, ought to have borders of gold, that is charity in all its brilliance. It should contain all the virtues and bring them together into unity. It should impart to one and all its own splendor and make the many into one, uniting with the many to the One, so that all may no longer be many but one.[23]

After this "aside" of oneness, Aelred quickly returns to a more practical tone:

> Now charity has two divisions, love of God and love of one's neighbor. Further, love of one's neighbor has two subdivisions, innocence and beneficence, that is, to do no harm to anyone and to do good to those to whom you are able. It is written: "What you would not have done to yourself do not to another" - and this is innocence. Our Lord says in the Gospel: "Everything that you would have men to to you, do you also to them" - this is beneficence.[24]

It is important to note that the Franciscan emphasis on "naughting" did not originate with St. Francis of Assisi. Aelred, quoting Gregory,[25] fervently advocates this utter dispossession to his sister, although he himself as abbot (hence steward) of flourishing Rievaulx could not practice complete disengagement from the material aspects of life. Also, Aelred was able, only occasionally,[26] to experience the delights of silence, of a contemplative way of life, for he was never free during his abbacy from administrative duties, the management of communal property, guidance of monks and lay people, the arbitration of disputes - the many demands of his abbatial office. Consequently, a life of contemplative devotion must have seemed doubly attractive to one who had to relinquish his innate attraction for an interior life, in order to fulfill his duties as "The Chimaera of the North".[27]

The concluding section of "Rule for a Recluse" is a "three-fold meditation" on the past (i.e. all the incidents of Jesus's life as recorded by the four evangelists), the present - in which Aelred congratulates his sister on the protective presence of God's grace in her life, and the future in which his imagined contemplation of the torments of hell and the joys of heaven anticipate Dante's Divine Comedy.

This type of discursive, three-fold meditation[28] is common in Aelred's writings and in that of his contemporaries and spiritual predecessors, as well.

One of the facets of Aelred's manner of presenting his "meditations" is his invitation to the reader to participate, through imagination and empathy, in bygone, sacred events and thus, in a sense, to experience them.

Aelred's meditation on the present includes autobiographical material that is not strictly germane to the "now" but which serves as a background to it. Aelred confesses his own proneness in early youth to the seductions and distractions of sensual pleasures and applauds his sister's escape from such snares.

However, Aelred's innate common sense asserts itself and he cautions his sister against the dangers of sanctimoniousness and smugness:

> So you exult in these riches which God's grace preserved for you, while I have the utmost difficulty in repairing what has been broken, recovering what has been lost, mending what has been torn. Yet in this respect I would have you emulate me. How you would blush if, after all my sins, I were found equal to you in the next life! The glory of virginity is often tarnished by vices which make their way in later on, while the reformation of a man's life and the replacement of vices by virtues can cancel the infamy of his former behavior.[29]

He concludes his meditation on the present with earnest exhortations that his sister be deeply mindful and grateful for God's grace in her life and that she sever her mind from all worldly attachments and anxieties. Aelred begs her to

> Let Him be your barn, your storecupboard, your purse, your wealth, your delight; let Him alone be all things in all.[30]

Aelred's meditation on the future involves imaginative depictions of medieval concepts of the after-life - the torments of the damned, the terror of those who are waiting to be judged and the beatitude of those who are saved. As mentioned earlier, the vividness of this "meditation" is a sketch, a prefiguration of Dante's epic canvas - The Divine Comedy.

Aelred's innate optimism asserts itself in the depiction of his vision of the messianic kingdom - a realm of ineffable bounty[31] and an epiphany of restoration on all levels. Aelred stresses the uniqueness of the Creator whose divine self-revelation he regards as His highest, most gracious gift.

> What is there further to seek? To be sure, what surpasses all these things, that is the sight, the knowledge and the love of the Creator. He will be seen in Himself, He will be seen in all His creatures, ruling everything without anxiety, upholding everything without toil, giving Himself and, so to speak, distributing Himself to one and all according to their capacity without any lessening or division of Himself. That lovable face, so longed for, upon which the angels yearn to gaze, will be seen. Who can say anything of its beauty, of its light, of its sweetness?...Hence there is born such love, such ardent affection, such sweetness of charity, such abundance of enjoyment, such vehement desire, that neither does satiety lessen desire nor

desire hinder satiety. What is this? To be sure, what eye has not seen nor ear heard, nor heart conceived, what God has prepared for those who love Him.[32]

Aelred's spiritual optimism is an intrinsic aspect of his faith in the loving, active presence of God in history and in the life of each of His creatures. Although the recent events of history have again raised perennial questions about God's omnipotence, Aelred's stubborn faith and persistent optimism (in spite of the carnality and carnage of his own times) remind one of the astonishing faith of the Hasidim[33] when trapped in one of the cruelest periods of (in) human history.

Notes to CHAPTER IX

1. A. Squire, Aelred of Rievaulx..., p. 119.

2. See David Knowles' introduction to Aelred's Treatises and Pastoral Prayer, p. xi.

3. Jerome, Ambrose, Gregory and Augustine. See A. Squire, Aelred of Rievaulx..., p. 120.

4. Aelred, "Rule of Life for a Recluse" in Treatises and Pastoral Prayer, pp. 46-47.

5. Ibid., pp. 93-96.

6. See A. Squire, Aelred of Rievaulx..., pp. 118-119:

   Aelred...may have had a feeling of special affinity with his sister's vocation to the life of solitude. In the world from which Aelred came this vocation was widely accepted and honoured, and no account of the religious life of the north of England in his day which only mentioned the features of change and the occasional troubles and scandals would be complete. There was a long continuity behind the attraction to the eremitical life. Not only had the great St. Cuthbert finished his life in solitude, but so had many others both before and since his day. In the eighth century St. John of Beverley had used a little anchorage just across the Tyne from Hexham. The Durham book of benefactors, which goes back to the ninth century, originally listed its donors in order of dignity, and in those lists the hermits come immediately after the kings and queens and before the abbots. At the time Aelred was writing, a Durham monk, Bartholomew, was once again living as a hermit on Cuthbert's Farne islands. But a closer and more personal contact was with the colourful Godric of Finchale, a friend and confidant of Aelred, who was instrumental in getting Godric's life written by Reginald of Durham. From this life we learn that Godric had his sister Burcwen living in an anchorhold chose at hand which he had himself built for her. She was evidently not completely enclosed, since she was able to attend Mass in Godric's oratory when he had a priest staying with him, as Aelred sometimes did. Of Aelred's own sister we know neither her name, nor the place where her cell was. We should expect it to be somewhere in the area between Hexham and Durham, most probably in a churchyard, but there were women with an attraction to solitude near York too and, when Aelred was still a young man, Archbishop Thurston had tried to persuade a notable recluse, Christina of Markyate near St. Albans, to come and take charge of his newly-founded community of nuns. She preferred to continue in solitude, but even there such women were neither isolated nor deprived of spiritual influence. Aelred's sister had, according to his own confession, waited a long time for him to write something for her, and was an anchoress of experience by the time she received a work which she had requested not just for herself, but for other younger women, whom she had encouraged to embrace this form of life, and to whom she was having to give counsel. Aelred was thus ensured of an audience of more than one, and in fact his work never ceased altogether to have some influence on English anchoresses throughout the Middle Ages.

7. Ibid., p. 128. Also see David Knowles' introduction to Aelred's *Treatises and Pastoral Prayer*, p. xii.

8. Chaucer, "The Summoner's Tale" in *Canterbury Tales*.

9. See Jerome, Epistle 22. Also see St. Ambrose, *Exhortatio Virginitatis*, c. 12, 72.

10. See A. Squire, *Aelred of Rievaulx...*, p. 120.

11. Knowles, Coleman, Squire.

12. See Chapter VII of this thesis.

13. See note 3, p. 46 in Aelred's *Treatises and Pastoral Prayer*.

14. See Giles Constable, "Aelred of Rievaulx and the nun of Watton: an episode in the early history of the Gilbertine order," in *Medieval Women*, ed. by Derek Baker (Oxford: Clarendon Press, 1978).

15. Aelred, "Rule of Life for a Recluse," pp. 93-96.

16. Ibid., p. 71.

17. Ibid., p. 70.

18. Ibid., p. 72.

19. See *Cloud of Unknowing*, trans. Ira Progoff (New York: York: Dell Pub. Co., Inc., 1957), pp. 102-115, pp. 175-176.

20. Aelred, *Spiritual Friendship*, p. 119-131.

21. See Aelred's "Rule of Life for a Recluse", pp. 77-78.

22. Ibid., p. 74.

23. Ibid.

24. Ibid., pp. 74-75.

25. St. Gregory, "Fifth Homily on the Gospel", n. 3.

26. See Aelred's "Jesus at the Age of Twelve", pp. 37-38.

27. See Douglas Roby, "Chimaera of the North: The Active Life of Aelred of Rievaulx" in *Cistercian Ideals and Reality*, pp. 152-169.

28. See David Knowles' introduction to Aelred's *Treatises and the Pastoral Prayer*, p. xi.

29. Aelred, "Rule of Life for a Recluse", pp. 95-96.

30. *Ibid.*, p. 97.

31. *Ibid.*, p. 101.

32. *Ibid.*, pp. 101-102.

33. See Yaffa Eliach, *Hasidic Tales of the Holocaust* (New York: Oxford University Press, 1982).

CHAPTER X

SOME RECENT RESPONSES TO THE CONTRIBUTION

OF AELRED OF RIEVAULX

Since the publication of Powicke's translation of Vita Ailredi in 1922, there has been a resurgence of interest in Aelred's work among some contemporary[1] medievalists, clerics, historians and lovers of literature. However, very few books have been published which focus exclusively on this abbot of Rievaulx.

Amedee Hallier's Un Educateur Monastique was originally published in Paris, in 1959. A decade later it was translated into English and published in Ireland (by the Cistercians), entitled The Monastic Theology of Aelred of Rievaulx.

Another book which gives us a great deal of insight into Aelred's life and work is A. Squire's Aelred of Rievaulx - A Study, which was first published in London, in 1969. Squire informs us that this book is the fruit of two decades of research and reflection.

David Knowles' comments about Aelred in <u>The Monastic Order in England</u> and his introduction to Aelred's <u>Treatises and the Pastoral Prayer</u> offer us valuable information and interesting perspectives.

Louis Bouyer's <u>The Cistercian Heritage</u> contains a lengthy, well-written chapter on Aelred of Rievaulx which adds to one's knowledge of Aelred's contribution as an author and as a pastor.

Adele Fiske, Douglas Roby, Thomas Merton and Charles Dumont have contributed articles and comments on <u>Spiritual Friendship</u>. The research of Powicke, Knowles, Southern and Squire have deepened and enriched scholars' understanding of Aelred's background, milieu, writings and contribution to medieval humanism.

The translations of Aelred's works by J. Dubois, G. Webb and A. Walker, Sisters Jerome, Paul and Eugenia, Father Theodore, A. Squire and C. Talbot have enabled many people who do not know Latin to appreciate and enjoy the books penned by this abbot of Rievaulx. Moreover, the commentaries of Dubois, Talbot, Webb and Walker, and A. Squire are very sound from a scholarly standpoint.

Articles by Odo Brooke, Alberic Stacpoole, Columban Heaney, Mary H. Veeder have contributed significantly to Aelredian scholarship. In this context, it is pertinent to mention the unpublished doctoral dissertation (Fordham

University, 1974) of Sister Marie Anne Mayeski. Entitled "Ailred of Rievaulx (1109-1167) and the Spiritual Life: A Study of the influence of Anthropology on Theology," this dissertation attempts to elucidate the thesis that "Ailred's notion of man is the determinative foundation which gives substance and coherence to his entire spiritual doctrine."

Although all the scholars mentioned above have enriched the field of Aelredian studies, the contributions of Powicke, Knowles and Squire deserve particular emphasis. John R. Sommerfeldt's two books on Aelred published in 2005 and 2006 are listed in the bibliography.

I know of no other Aelredian scholar of the 20th century who has invested as much time and energy in the quest of Aelred of Rievaulx as his namesake and co-religionist, Aelred Squire. Fascinated by the gracious geniality of this abbot of Rievaulx, Squire was initially intrigued and consequently inspired by Aelred's ability to remain rooted in a compassionate catholicity of spirit in spite of the cruelty and carnage of the age in which he lived. Centuries ahead of his time, Aelred did not regard women as inferior to men, nor did he advocate or endorse the medieval crusades against the "infidels." Rooted in his faith in the strength of <u>caritas</u>, Aelred resolved to instruct by example rather than rhetoric. Under his abbacy, Rievaulx became a flourishing sanctuary[2] where no one was refused admittance, respect, affection and affirmation as a fellow human being. This friend and confidante[3] of kings, popes and bishops also succeeded in evoking the love[4] and loyalty of anonymous monks and illiterate laity. His secret was a simple one. Convinced of the immanence of grace, he regarded human beings as confrères, as fellow-pilgrims engaged in a common quest for Truth.

The testimony of his contemporaries[5] suggests that Aelred's buoyancy of spirit, his contagious <u>caritas</u> inspired, consoled and occasionally angered those who sought his counsel and company. Perhaps the words of the late Professor David Knowles (who was himself a compatriot and a co-religionist of Aelred) best sums up this essay/study of the humanism of Aelred of Rievaulx.

> Ailred has been called "the Bernard of the North," and he resembles his great master in several ways, in his multifarious activities, pastoral, literary, administrative, and in his sermons and letters. Like Bernard he is in many ways a contradiction of the Cistercian program of solitude, silence and anonymity; like Bernard he remained true to his monastic observance amid both activity and infirmity. There are nevertheless many differences. Ailred, with all his gifts, was not a universal genius of the calibre of Bernard, nor was he a writer or thinker of equal power and versatility. He was not a doctor of the Church, nor the hammer of popes and deliquent bishops. His was a pure and steady candle-flame; not a blaze that could light up a dark sky or consume a forest. Yet he had a personality unique among the writers and abbots of that age. Highly gifted, strong both to do and to suffer, he was an abbot whose wisdom appeared primarily in his personal love and sympathy and his wise direction of souls. As his disciple and biographer could say: he who loved us all was deeply loved by us in return, and counted this the greatest of all his blessings...[6]
> ...Gentleness, radiance of affection and wide sympathy are not the qualities which most would associate with the early Cistercians, but they are assuredly the outstanding natural characteristics of Ailred...No other English monk of the twelfth century so lingers in the memory; like Anselm of Bec, he escapes from his age, though most typical of it and speaks directly to us... of his restless search for One to whom he might give the full strength of his love."[7]

Notes to CHAPTER X

1. See the bibliography.

2. See Walter Daniel's *Vita Ailredi*, pp. 36, 38.

3. *Ibid*.

4. *Ibid*., pp. 3, 42.

5. *Ibid*., p. 59. Also see Aelred's *Spiritual Friendship*, p. 112.

6. See David Knowles' introduction to Aelred's *Treatises and the Pastoral Prayer*, pp. x-xi.

7. See David Knowles, *The Monastic Order in England*, pp. 242, 240.

APPENDIX

THREE MEDIEVAL LAMENTS

These laments express the anguish of three medieval Englishmen - Aelred of Rievaulx, Gilbert of Hoilandia and Jocelin of Furness.

Aelred was bemoaning the loss of his friend Simon[1] in the Mirror of Charity, Gilbert and Jocelin were lamenting the death of Aelred of Rievaulx.

Louis Bouyer in The Cistercian Heritage observes that Aelred's lament for Simon in the Mirror of Charity emphasizes the "place for human affection"[2] in the works of this abbot of Rievaulx. Although Aelred was acquainted with both classical[3] and Christian[4] eulogies, the following paragraphs seem to express the vivid grief of personal loss:

> But sorrow forbids me to go on, for the recent death of my Simon forces me to weep for sorrow. Perhaps this is what makes me wake at night, quaking with fear.

Perhaps it is because my dearest friend was taken out
of this life so soon, that nightmares deprive me of
the few hours' sleep I need. No wonder that I was confused and disturbed before this sudden death; my soul
must have had a presentiment that he whose life had filled
me with such joy and delight, was soon to be taken from
me. And now what I feared so much has happened. Why
have I tried to hide my feelings, and refused to talk
about my sorrow? It is probably because I have kept
silent that I am still so upset. But I must let the
tears out of my eyes and the sobs from my lips, and
show the sorrow buried deep within my heart. Then perhaps, by talking about Simon's death and weeping over him,
my heart may rid itself of its burden.

Have pity on me, if you are my friends, now that God's
hand has fallen on me. And if you are surprised to
see me weeping, you should be even more surprised to
see me still alive. The only one who would not be astonished to see Aelred living without Simon, would be
someone who did not know how pleasant it was for us to
spend our life on earth together; how great a joy it
would have been for us to journey to heaven in each
other's company...

Do you remember how bitterly Jacob wept when he saw
Joseph's bloodstained coat, and thought that he was
dead? Think how, when Jacob died, Joseph threw himself
down beside the bed, weeping and covering his father's
face with kisses. Imagine how David wept at the death
of his friend Jonathan, whom he had loved more than any
woman. Why then, have I not the right to weep for Simon,
who meant just as much to me? He was my son in age,
my father in his example of holiness, my friend in godly
love...What do I care if streams of tears flow from
my eyes throughout the day and night? Weep then, not
because Simon has been taken up to heaven, but because
Aelred has been left on earth, alone.[5]

Douglas Roby[6] informs us that Gilbert, abbot of Hoilandia

(Swineshead) in Lincolnshire "broke off his sermon in chapter

to make a moving eulogy when the news of Aelred's death was

brought:

> Within the last few days, a very rich honeycomb has
> been carried into the unending banquet of heaven, for
> as we were speaking about the words: "I ate honey in
> its comb and drank wine mixed with milk", news arrived

of the death of the Lord Abbot of Rievaulx...Who else has led a life as pure as Aelred's? Whose advice was ever so full of discretion? I doubt whether there has ever been a man whose mind remained so quick and nimble, while his body was so crippled by bad health. From his lips words of wisdom flowed as smoothly as honey from its comb. As he grew weaker through ill health, the spirit within him pined more and more with love and desire for the things of heaven. His flesh was the myrrh, his mind the fragrant spices, his desire the undying flame of the sweet incense that he offered each day in his ceaseless longing to see God face to face. And as his body wasted away, his soul waxed strong as if fed on the food from some rich feast. His mouth sang praises to the Lord in tones of joy as sweet as honey dripping from its comb. His personality showed itself in his conversation, whilst the calmness of his face and even his very posture were evidence of his peace of soul. Although his sensitivity was of the keenest, he was never hasty or rash in voicing his opinion. He asked favours very unassumingly and granted them with the greatest of kindness. He would put up with annoyances caused by others, but he himself was a nuisance to none. His insight was penetrating, his judgements were the fruit of careful consideration, and his patience enabled him to bear with everything. I remember how it would often happen that one of the brethren clustering round him would interrupt some discourse that Aelred had begun, and the Abbot would wait until the brother had said all he had to say. And when the torrent of words had died away, Aelred would start again from where he had left off, speaking with that calmness and even temper which had allowed him to hold up the flow of his own thought, talking and pausing at just the right moments for his words to take their full effect. He himself was always ready to listen to others, and slow to assert his own opinion. And if I cannot say that he was slow to lose his temper, it is because that would be tantamount to saying that he did sometimes lose his temper; but in fact he never did.[7]

Jocelin of Furness wrote his Life of St. Waldef (Waldef was the boyhood friend of Aelred and his confrère in religious life) forty years after the demise of Aelred of Rievaulx.[8] However, Jocelin's portrait of Aelred also imparts an "impression of tranquility and forbearance"[9] which is conveyed by the lament of Gilbert of Hoilandia. Jocelin stated that

> He (Aelred) was a man of fine old English stock (ex ueterum Anglorum illustri stirpe procreatus). He left school early and was brought up from boyhood in the court of King David with Henry the king's son and Waldef. In course of time he became first a monk, afterwards abbot of Rievaulx. His school learning was slight, but as a result of careful self-discipline in the exercise of his acute natural powers, he was cultured above many who have been thoroughly trained in secular learning. He drilled himself in the study of Holy Scripture, and left a lasting memorial behind him in writings distinguished by their lucid style, and wealth of edifying instruction, for he was wholly inspired by a spirit of wisdom and understanding. Moreover, he was a man of the highest integrity, of great practical wisdom, witty and eloquent, a pleasant companion, generous and discreet. And, with all these qualities, he exceeded all his fellow prelates of the Church in his patience and tenderness. He was full of sympathy for the infirmities, both physical and moral, of others.[10]

Notes to the APPENDIX

1. See Powicke's introduction to Vita Ailredi, p. lxvi.

2. Louis Bouyer, The Cistercian Heritage (London: A. R. Mowbray and Co., Ltd., 1958), p. 138.

3. A. Squire, Aelred of Rievaulx...p. 82.

4. Ibid.

5. Aelred, Mirror of Charity, chapter 34 (cols. 539-41), trans. by Geoffry Webb and Adrian Walker. Quoted by L. Bouyer in The Cistercian Heritage, pp. 130-131.

6. See Douglas Roby's introduction to Aelred's Spiritual Friendship, p. 14.

7. Gilbert of Hoilandia's lament for Aelred is quoted by L. Bouyer in *The Cistercian Heritage*, pp. 130-131. Trans. by Geoffry Webb and Adrian Walker.

8. See David Knowles' *The Monastic Order in England*, p. 645.

    Jocelin wrote his *Vita S. Waldeni* during c. 1210-14. Aelred had passed away in c. 1167.

9. See Powicke's introduction to *Vita Ailredi*, p. xxxiii.

10. *Ibid*. Trans. by F. M. Powicke.

BIBLIOGRAPHY

Sources

Aelred of Rievaulx, De Spirituali Amicitia: Dubois, J., ed., L'amitie spirituelle, Latin text translation, notes (Bruges: C. Beyaert, 1948).

Hoste, A., ed. De Spirituali Amicitia, critical edition, CCM 1: 287-350, Magna Bibliotheca Veterum Patrum (Cologne, 1618) vol. 13, pp. 129-143.

Maxima Bibliotheca Veterum Patrum (Lyons), 1677) vol. 33., pp. 138-153.

Migne, J. P., ed., Beati Aelredi Abbatis Rievallensis Opera Omnia (Paris, 1855) PL 195:659-702

Tissier, B., ed. Bibliotheca Patrum Cisterciensium (Bonnefontaine, 1662) vol. 5, pp.362-380.

Ambrose of Milan, De Offciis Ministrorum, ed., J. P. Migne (Paris, 1845) PL 16: 28-184.

Cassian, J., Conferences, ed., E. Pichery, Conferences, 3 vols., SCH 42, 54, 64 (Paris: Cerf, 1955-1959), Conference 16: De Amicitia, 2: 221-247.

Cicero, Marcus Tullius, De Senectute-De Amicitia-De Divinatione, Latin text, translation, W. Falconer (New York: Putnam, 1922).

Daniel, Walter, Vita Ailredi Abbatis Reivall', Latin text, and English translation. Ed. and trans. by F. M. Powicke (N.Y.: Oxford University Press, 1951). 2nd ed., (Oxford: Clarendon Press, 1978).

Books by Aelred of Rievaulx

De Spirituali Amicitia, ed., J. Dubois (Bruges: Baeyaert, 1948);

Spiritual Friendship, translated by Mary Eugenia Laker (Cistercian Fathers Series, 5., Kalamazoo, Michigan, 1977).

Tractatus de Anima, ed., C. H. Talbot (London: Warburg Institute, 1952).

Dialogue on the Soul, translated by C. H. Talbot (Cistercian Fathers Series, 22., Kalamazoo, Michigan, 1981).

De Institutione Inclusarum, ed., C. H. Talbot in *Analecta Sacri Ordinis Cisterciensis*, VII (1951) pp. 167-217; "Rule for a Recluse" in *The Works of Aelred of Rievaulx*, vol. 1., (Cistercian Fathers Series, 2., Spencer, Mass., 1971).

"Rule of Life for a Recluse" in *Treatises and the Pastoral Prayer*, 2nd. ed. (Kalamazoo, Michigan: Cistercian Publications, Inc., 1982).

Tractatus de Jesu puero duodenni, ed., A. Hoste (Paris: Cerf, 1958), *Sources Chrétiennes*, No. 60; "When Jesus Was Twelve" in *The Works of Aelred of Rievaulx*, vol. 1., (Cistercian Father Series, 2., Spencer, Mass., 1971).

"Jesus at the Age of Twelve" in *Treatises and the Pastoral Prayer*, 2nd. ed. (Kalamazoo, Michigan: Cistercian Publications, Inc., 1982).

Oratio Pastoralis, ed., C. Dumont (Paris: Cerf, 1961), *Sources Chretiennes*, No. 76; "The Pastoral Prayer" in *The Works of Aelred of Rievaulx*, vol. 1 (Cistercian Fathers Series, 2., Spencer, Mass., 1971).

Sermones Inediti, ed., C. H. Talbot (Rome: S. O. Cisterciensis, 1952).

Speculum Caritatis, *Patrologiae cursus completus, series Latina*, E., J. P. Migne (Paris, 1878-1890) P. L. 195, 504-620.

Mirror of Charity translated by G. Webb and A. Walker (London: Mowbray, 1962).

Studies

Barratt, Alexandra, "'De Institutione Inclusarum' of Aelred of Rievaulx and the Carthusian Order" in *Journal of Theological Studies*, 1977.

Bouyer, Louis, *The Cistercian Heritage*, tr., E. Livingston, London: Mowbray, 1958.

-- *Christian Humanism*, Westminster, Md., Newman, 1959.

Broderick, J., "St. Aelred, Abbot of Rievaulx" in *The Clergy Review*, 26 (1946) pp. 27-36.

Brooke, Odo, *Studies in Monastic Theology*, Kalamazoo, Michigan: Cistercian Publications, Inc. 1980.

Bynum, Caroline W., "Cistercian conception of community: an aspect of twelfth century spirituality" in *Harvard Theological Review*, 1975.

-- *Jesus as Mother*, Los Angeles: University of California Press, 1982.

Chenu, M. D., *Nature, Man and Society in the Twelfth Century*, Chicago: The University of Chicago Press, 1968.

Anonymous *The Cloud of Unknowing*, tr., Ira Progoff, New York: Dell Publishing Co., Inc., 1957.

Constable, Giles, "Aelred of Rievaulx and the nun of Watton: an episode in the early history of the Gilbertine Order", in *Medieval Women*, ed. by Derek Baker, Oxford, 1978.

Dumont, C., "Aelred de Rievaulx" in *Theologie de la vie monastique*, Paris: Aubier, 1961, pp. 527-538.

-- "St. Aelred: The Balanced Life of the Monk" in *Monastic Studies*, 1, (1963), pp. 23-58.

-- Aelred of Rievaulx's *Spiritual Friendship*, in Cistercian *Ideals and Reality*. Ed., John Sommerfeldt, Cistercian Publications, Kalamazoo, Michigan, 1978.

Easwaran, Eknath, *Gandhi the Man*, San Francisco: Glide Publications, 1975.

Eliach, Yaffa, *Hasidic Tales of the Holocaust*, New York: Oxford University Press, 1982.

Fiske, A., *Friends and Friendship in the Monastic Tradition*, Chapter 18, "Aelred of Rievaulx." Cidoc Cuaderno 51. Cuernavaca: CIDOC, Mexico, 1970.

Fraser, Antonia,   The lives of the kings and queens of England, New York: Alfred A. Knopf, Inc., 1975.

Gilson, E.,   The Mystical Theology of St. Bernard, New York: Sheed and Ward, 1940.

Hallier, A.,   The Monastic Theology of Aelred of Rievaulx: An Experiential Theology, CS 2, Spencer, Mass.,: Cistercian Publications, 1969. (Introduction by Thomas Merton).

Harvey, T. E.,   St. Aelred of Rievaulx, London, 1932

Haskins, C. H.,   The Renaissance of the Twelfth Century, Cambridge: Harvard University Press, 1927.

Heaney, C.,   "Aelred of Rievaulx: his relevance to the post-Vatican II age", in The Cistercian Spirit, ed., M. Basil Pennington, Cistercian Studies 3, (Spencer, Mass., 1970), pp. 166-189.

Hoste, A.,   Bibliotheca Aelrediana, Steenbrugge: Sint Petersabdij, 1962.

Hunt, W.,   "Ethelred" in Dictionary of National Biography, 6 (1908), pp. 897f.

Jarret, B.,   "Aelred" in The English Way, ed., M. Ward. New York: Sheed and Ward, 1933, pp. 81-103.

Knowles, D.,   "The Humanism of the Twelfth Century" in his The Historian and Character, (Cambridge, England, 1963), pp. 16-30.

--   The Monastic Order in England, (2nd. ed., Cambridge, England, 1963).

--   Introduction to Aelred's Treatises and the Pastoral Prayer, 2nd. ed., Kalamazoo, Michigan: Cistercian Publications, 1982.

Lang, A.,   The History of Scotland, Vol. I., New York: Dodd, Mead, and Co., 1901.

Leclercq, J.,   The love of learning and the desire for God, Fordham University Press, New York, 1961.

Lepp, I., *The Ways of Friendship*, New York: Macmillan 1966.

Louth, A., *The Origins of the Christian Mystical Tradition*, Oxford: Clarendon Press, 1981.

Mayeski, Marie Anne, *Ailred of Rievaulx (1109-1167) and the spiritual life: a study of the influence of anthropology on theology.* Unpublished dissertation, Fordham University, 1974.

McNamara, Sr., M.A., *Friends and Friendship for St. Augustine.* Staten Island: Alba House, 1964.

Miles, Margaret, "Vision: The Eye of the Body and the Eye of the Mind in Saint Augustine's De Trinitate and Confessions," reprinted in 1983 by the University of Chicago from *The Journal of Religion*, Vol. 63, No. 2, April, 1983.

Pedrick, D. "Some Reflections on St. Aelred of Rievaulx" in *Buckfast Abbey Chronicle*, 14 (1944) pp. 10-25.

Powicke, F. M., *Ailred of Rievaulx and his biographer Walter Daniel.* Manchester: Longmans Green & Co., 1922.

-- Introduction to Walter Daniel's *Vita Ailredi*, Oxford: Clarendon Press, 1978.

Raciti, Gaetano. "L'apport original d'Aelred de Rievaulx a la reflexion occidentale sur l'amitie" in *Collectanea Cisterciensia*, 29 (1967) pp. 77-99.

Roby, Douglas, "Chimaera of the North: the active life of Aelred of Rievaulx" in *Cistercian Ideals and Reality*. Ed. by John Sommerfeldt. Cistercian Publications, Kalamazoo, Michigan, 1978.

-- Introduction to Aelred's *Spiritual Friendship*, trans, by Mary Eugenia Laker, Kalamazoo, Michigan: Cistercian Publications, 1977.

Schilling, R., "Aelredus von Rievaulx: Deus Amicitia est" in *Citeaux in de Nederlanden*, 8 (1957) pp. 13-26.

Southern, R. W., *Medieval Humanism.* Oxford: Basil Blackwell, 1970.

Squire, A. *Aelred of Rievaulx: A Study*. London: SPCK, 1969.

-- *Aelred of Rievaulx: A Study*. 2nd ed., Kalamazoo, Michigan: Cistercian Publications, 1981.

-- "Aelred of Rievaulx and the Monastic Tradition concerning Action and Contemplation" in *Downside Review*, 72 (1954), pp,. 289-303.

Stacpoole, A., "The Public Face of Aelred", *Downside Review* 85 (1967), pp,. 183-199, 318-325.

Veeder, Mary Harris. "Negation and Apocalypse: Style and Vision in Aelred of Rievaulx" in *Cistercian Ideals and Reality*, Ed. by John R. Sommerfeldt. Kalamazoo, Michigan: Cistercian Publications, 1978.

Further Secondary Sources.

Burton, Janet. "The Estates and Economy of Rievaulx Abbey in Yorkshire." Citeaux Commentarii cistercienses 49 (1998), pp. 29-94.

Dumont. Charles. " Aelred of Rievaulx ; His Life and Works." Trans. Elizabeth Connor. Cistercian Fathers 17. Kalamazoo, Michigan : Cistercian Publications 1990, pp. 11-67.

Dutton, Marsha L. " Aelred, Historian : Two Portraits in Plantagenet Myth." Cistercian Studies Quarterly 28 (1993) pp. 113-143.

-- -- "Aelred of Rievaulx on Friendship, Chastity and Sex : The Sources." Cistercian Studies Quarterly 29 (1994) pp.121-196.

La Corte, Daniel M. " The Abbatial Concerns of Aelred of Rievaulx ..." Cistercian Studies Quarterly 30 (1995), pp. 267-73.

McGinn, Bernard. *The Growth of Mysticism.The Presence of God. A History of Western Mysticism...*New York : Crossroad, 1994.

McGuire, Brian Patrick. *Friendship and Community : The Monastic Experience : 350-1250*. Cistercian Studies 95. Kalamazoo, Michigan. Cistercian Publications Inc., 1988.

-- -- *Brother and Lover : Aelred of Rievaulx*. New York : Crossroad, 1994.

Newman, Martha G. *The Boundaries of Charity : Cistercian Culture and Ecclesiastical Reform*. pp. 1098-1180. Reading Medieval Culture. Stanford, CA. Stanford University Press, 1996.

Renna, Thomas. " Moses in the Writings of Aelred of Rievaulx." Citeaux Commentarii cistercensis 46, pp.111-125. (1995).

Sommerfeldt, John R. " The Roots of Aelred's Spirituality : Cosmology and Anthropology." Cistercian Studies Quarterly 38 (2003) pp.19-26.

-- -- *Aelred of Rievaulx : Pursuing Perfect Happiness*. New York/ Mahwah, N. J. The Newman Press, 2005.

--. -- *Aelred of Rievaulx : On Love and Order in the World and the Church*. New York/Mahwah, N.J.: The Newman Press, 2006.

Te Pas, Katherine. " Spiritual Friendship in Alered of Rievaulx and Mutual Sanctification in Marriage." Cistercian Studies Quarterly 27 (1992) pp.63-76, pp.153-165.

Yohe, Katherine (nee Te Pas). " Adhering to a Friend in the Spirit of Christ. "Cistercian Studies Quarterly 33 (1998) pp.29-44.

www.ingramcontent.com/pod-product-compliance
Lightning Source LLC
Chambersburg PA
CBHW081216230426
43666CB00015B/2751